'In 2022, Kate Bush's 'Running Up That Hill (A Deal with God)' was discovered by a new generation of listeners, largely due to its use in the TV series *Stranger Things*. Stephen Glynn's book provides a timely and insightful look at the ways in which Bush has engaged with visual media.'
Dr Paul Newland, *University of Worcester*

'Sitting across music, video and film, *Kate Bush and the Moving Image* is a welcome new study of this important British artist. Stephen Glynn expertly weaves together close readings of Bush's music and her work as a video artist with an account of their cultural contexts and heritage. Glynn's knowledge of popular culture is remarkable in its range and depth. An innovative book on an innovative artist.'
James Chapman, *University of Leicester*

Kate Bush and the Moving Image

In this unique study, Stephen Glynn demonstrates that Kate Bush's work, in both sound and vision, has long been influenced and characterised by, and at times aimed at, film and television media.

The volume explores in depth Bush's 'music of allusion' and analyses first the significance of film and television references throughout the lyrics and settings of her songs, beginning with her breakthrough hit 'Wuthering Heights'. It also surveys the shaping presence of film and television in the look, narrative and artistry of her music videos, including the examination of celebrated works such as 'Cloudbusting' and 'Hounds of Love'. Finally, the book assesses Bush's most intensive cinematic undertaking, her 1993 album *The Red Shoes*, with its evident homage to the 1948 film of Michael Powell and Emeric Pressburger, and its concurrent visual reworking as Bush's sole film venture, *The Line, The Cross & The Curve*. Thus, with its deployment across music, video and film, Glynn demonstrates the centrality of Kate Bush's cinephilia to her work.

Accessible yet academically rigorous, *Kate Bush and the Moving Image* is a stand-out study of the iconic singer-songwriter's discography and cinematic ventures. It will appeal to both students and scholars of Film, Television, Media, Cultural and Popular Music Studies.

Stephen Glynn lectures in Film at Television at De Montfort University, UK. His previous investigations of the interconnections between pop music performers and the visual media include *David Bowie and Film* (2022), *The Beatles and Film* (2021), *Cultographies: Quadrophenia* (2014) and *The British Pop Music Film* (2013).

Kate Bush and the Moving Image

Stephen Glynn

Routledge
Taylor & Francis Group
LONDON AND NEW YORK

First published 2025
by Routledge
4 Park Square, Milton Park, Abingdon, Oxon OX14 4RN

and by Routledge
605 Third Avenue, New York, NY 10158

Routledge is an imprint of the Taylor & Francis Group, an informa business

© 2025 Stephen Glynn

The right of Stephen Glynn, to be identified as author of this work has been asserted in accordance with sections 77 and 78 of the Copyright, Designs and Patents Act 1988.

All rights reserved. No part of this book may be reprinted or reproduced or utilised in any form or by any electronic, mechanical, or other means, now known or hereafter invented, including photocopying and recording, or in any information storage or retrieval system, without permission in writing from the publishers.

Trademark notice: Product or corporate names may be trademarks or registered trademarks, and are used only for identification and explanation without intent to infringe.

British Library Cataloguing-in-Publication Data
A catalogue record for this book is available from the British Library

Library of Congress Cataloging-in-Publication Data
A catalog record has been requested for this book

ISBN: 978-1-032-76684-3 (hbk)
ISBN: 978-1-032-76686-7 (pbk)
ISBN: 978-1-003-47960-4 (ebk)

DOI: 10.4324/9781003479604

Typeset in Times New Roman
by Taylor & Francis Books

For Sarah and Roz

Contents

List of figures xi
Acknowledgements xii

1 Introduction: Kate Bush and Swapping Places 1

PART 1
Music 15

2 It's Like a Film: Kate Bush and Songs Influenced by Screen Media 17

3 Be Kind to My Mistakes: Kate Bush and Bespoke Soundtrack Work 37

PART 2
Video 47

4 Moments of Pleasure: Kate Bush as Music Video Performer 49

5 This Woman's Work: Kate Bush as Music Video Director 63

PART 3
Film 83

6 A Matter of Life and Death: Kate Bush and *The Red Shoes* 85

7 Strange Phenomena: Kate Bush and *The Line, The Cross & The Curve* 98

8 Conclusion: Kate Bush and the Whole Story 125

Appendix: Kate Bush's Desert Island Films 130
Videography 133
Bibliography 136
Index 141

Figures

1.1	*Stranger Things* – 'It Doesn't Hurt Me'.	2
2.1	'Wuthering Heights' – Window Dressing.	19
2.2	'Hammer Horror' – Fingers and Thumbs.	23
2.3	'Delius (Song of Summer)' – Bush's Swan Song.	26
2.4	'There Goes a Tenner' – Bush Goes to Ealing.	30
3.1	*She's Having a Baby* – 'It's Hard on the Man' (Discuss).	40
3.2	*Les Dogs* – The Bride Wore White.	45
4.1	'Army Dreamers' – The Boy in the Bush.	52
4.2	'Breathing' – The Girl in the Bubble.	54
4.3	'Running Up That Hill' – Lost in the Bush.	57
4.4	'Cloudbusting' – The Bush in the Boy.	60
5.1	'Hounds of Love' – 'I Don't Know What's Good for Me'.	65
5.2	'Experiment IV' – The Sound Siren.	69
5.3	'Rocket Man' – Bush meets Bowie.	72
5.4	'Deeper Understanding' – Bush meets Beckett.	75
5.5	'Wild Man' – Bush meets Yeti Hunters.	77
5.6	'And Dream of Sheep (Live)' – A Late Resurfacing.	79
6.1	'Lily' – Angel Eyes.	93
6.2	'You're the One' – Looking at The Big Skye.	96
7.1	*The Red Shoes* – Total Film.	102
7.2	*The Line, The Cross & The Curve* – Bush Meets Chaplin.	108
7.3	*The Line, The Cross & The Curve* – 'We Let the Weirdness In'.	111
7.4	*The Line, The Cross & The Curve* – Death and the Maiden.	116
7.5	*The Line, The Cross & The Curve* – 'I Can't Go On: I'll Go On'.	118
7.6	*The Line, The Cross & The Curve* – Music as the Food of Love.	121

Acknowledgements

Since my teenage years the work of Kate Bush has brought me innumerable moments of pleasure. She is a key artist in both sound and vision who merits rigorous analysis (rather than uncritical fandom) and this book is my appraisal and acknowledgement of her importance. To that end, my great thanks to Natalie Foster, Deanna Waistell and Daniela Amodeo at Routledge, who have expertly guided and supported this book from initial proposal to final production, always willing to be kind to my mistakes. My thanks to colleagues at De Montfort's Cinema and Television History Institute, whom I have found to be wonderful teachers and very good company. My thanks also to Sam Schorb and Roz Harrison for their invaluable assistance and deeper understanding on those taxing technological matters. Finally, for their unwavering encouragement and infectious belief that something good is going to happen, all the love, as ever, to Sarah and Roz.

1 Introduction
Kate Bush and Swapping Places

Kate Bush and *Stranger Things*

There was an appropriateness in the channels through which, in summer 2022, the music of British singer-songwriter Kate Bush was discovered by a new generation of listeners, and her single 'Running Up That Hill (A Deal with God)' topped numerous charts 37 years after its initial release. The song had first appeared on 5 August 1985 as the lead single from her *Hounds of Love* album, reaching number 3 in the UK charts, and number 30 on the Billboard Hot 100 (thus becoming Bush's first US top 30 hit). It unexpectedly came back to international attention when used at various points in the fourth season of Matt and Ross Duffer's Netflix science fiction-horror series *Stranger Things* (2016–), set during the 1980s in the fictional town of Hawkins, Indiana. In particular, 'Chapter 4: Dear Billy' (tx. 27 May 2022), an episode taking place in March 1986, sees Max Mayfield (Sadie Sink), investigating the mysterious deaths of several teenagers, become possessed by their murderer, a skeletal being known as Vecna (Jamie Campbell Bower) that inhabits the alternative reality of the Upside Down. Max's friends learn that music can break Vecna's hold on its prey and so they play on loop Max's favourite song, the one she constantly replayed on her Walkman, Bush's 'Running Up That Hill' (Figure 1.1). The strategy works, as the anthemic ballad with its thrumming synths, pounding snare drum and heaving Fairlight strings opens a portal to the Upside Down which allows Max, narrowly, to escape back to the real world and her friends. Bush, notoriously spartan in allowing the licencing of her music, was an avowed fan of the show and, with its significance explained by the show's runners, readily agreed to its use. The song was not just temporally apposite but also narratively, emotionally and thematically integrated. It possessed what

DOI: 10.4324/9781003479604-1

2 *Introduction*

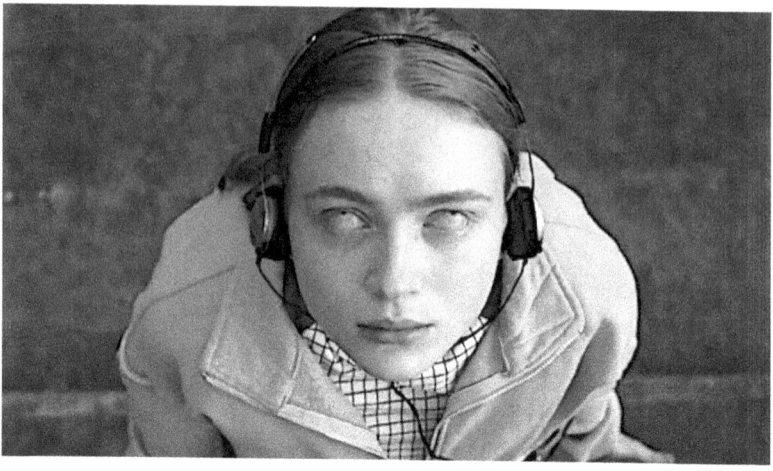

Figure 1.1 Stranger Things – 'It Doesn't Hurt Me'.

the Duffer brothers termed 'that cinematic build' to accompany Max's running up to the light and freedom (cited in Powers 2022), while its employment adhered to the song's premise of 'swapping places' since Max's friends must empathise fully with her feelings and predicament in order to provide the correct musical armour to liberate her.

Stranger Things brought a whole new awareness of Bush and her work: since 'Running Up That Hill' is diegetically employed, Bush is named several times throughout season four, as when Max's on-off boyfriend Lucas Sinclair (Caleb McLaughlin) confirms himself another firm fan. Empirically, the song topped the UK singles charts on 17 June 2022 and stayed there for three weeks, making Bush, aged 63, the oldest female artist to achieve such as feat. It also went to number one for seven weeks in Ireland, nine weeks in Australia and, as well as topping charts in several European countries, reached a new high of number 3 in the United States. In addition to enjoying a summer peak of 6 million daily streams on Spotify, by August 2022 the song surpassed 100 million views on YouTube. More pervasively, the series brought Bush back into youth culture as the song's fresh context, promising self-identity, hope and resilience, created a wave of retrospective fandom (including an estimated 140,000 Kate Bush-themed videos on TikTok's social media platform).

This re-discovery was not confined to a generation of American tweenagers, as I experienced at first hand. In Britain, not only was 'Running

Up That Hill' suddenly a near-constant presence on my satellite tv music channels and a regular on my gym's public playlist, but film studies students who had sat impassively while I lectured on Italian Neo-Realism and Jean-Luc Godard or surreptitiously looked down at their phones when I digressed into discussions of screen appearances by the Beatles and David Bowie, were now fully engaged by my work on the interconnectedness of film and popular music and enthusiastically asked questions about Bush. What did 'Running Up That Hill' mean? What else could I recommend? What other soundtracks had she done? They too had undertaken research and shared their recommendations, several enlighteningly raised from the backwaters of Bush's oeuvre. Again swapping places, the teacher had, at times, become the student.[1]

One thing I was able to stress to my charges was the serendipity in their discovery, and the depths their research could reach: Bush's music, I showed them, has long been influenced and characterised by (and at times aimed at) film and television media. Beginning with the television inspiration for 'Wuthering Heights', the song that brought her to international attention as a 19-year-old in 1978, the moving image has not just bookended Bush's career to date, but been a constant – and formative – presence in her work. Allied to her financially comfortable, well-educated upbringing where creativity was encouraged and with artistic older siblings, Bush was not just musically prodigious (writing songs from the age of 11) but visually voracious: 'I wasn't off reading books,' she has said of her childhood pastimes, 'I was watching television, and cinema' (*Profiles in Rock*, CITY-TV Canada, December 1980). Her intention was always to marry music with image, and from the off her management agreed: EMI's UK General Manager Bob Mercer, who signed Bush and funded her development from the age of 16 (Bush left school with ten 'O' levels), lauded her as 'a completely audio-visual artist' and told of the company's aim to break Bush in America not through traditional radio channels but (and this in the pre-MTV era) via television (Reynolds 2016: 577).[2] This monograph aims fully to explore this enduring symbiosis of music and the moving image, from individual references to shaping influences, and onto the screen-driven effect on her sole film release, 1993's *The Line, The Cross & The Curve*, created as an audio-visual adjunct to her seventh studio album, *The Red Shoes*, itself titled after and inspired by the 1948 British feature film from Michael Powell and Emeric Pressburger.

Kate Bush and the Starman

Alongside the late influence of *Stranger Things*, one can profitably underpin Bush's career with her shaping 'strange fascination' for a fellow multimedia artist.[3] As noted by Bonnie Gordon, Bush is not in the tradition of confessional singer-songwriters such as Joni Mitchell or Tori Amos, who create in the listener the sense of sharing directly the singer's personal experiences. This is not to suggest that Bush fails to draw on her own experiences but, 'instead of telling a story about herself, Bush takes inspiration from feelings, gestures, and pre-existent stories that provide moulds for articulating her experience' (2005: 38). Thus, rather than adopting the confessional mode, Bush constructs elaborate personae in her compositions, with her performative mode and range of voice allowing her to adopt a heterogeneous subjectivity that crosses gender, time, space and shape as she moves from her debut nineteenth-century Gothic heroine ('Wuthering Heights'), through *The Dreaming* and its ruthless Viet Cong soldier ('Pull Out the Pin'), and on even to the lifecycle of a snowflake ('Snowflake') in *50 Words for Snow*.

While her determination to avoid intrusive questions about her personal life made Bush an increasingly reluctant interviewee – and gained her unofficial titles such as 'rock's Stanley Kubrick' (John Aizlewood, 'The Big Sleep, *Q*, 185, December 2001) or the 'Greta Garbo of Pop' (Jovanovic 2005: 191) – she has always proved enlightening when addressing her work. For instance, Bush declared early how, 'When I perform, I'm definitely someone else. She's a lot stronger and I wouldn't be as daring as her.' In the same interview Bush cited a fellow chameleon singer-songwriter and his 'constructions' as a major influence – David Bowie. After praising Bowie's 'insect-like beauty', she lauded how 'He's always exploring, and he's very clever as a performer' ('Kate Bush: learning to sing and defying conventions', *Radio and Record News*, February 1978). As well as both hailing from edge-of-south-London suburbia (Welling versus Bromley), the overall equivalence between the artistic practice of Bush and Bowie has been regularly cited. Tom Doyle notes their shared 'creative bravery and shapeshifting characteristics' (2022: 44), while Simon Reynolds inventories how, through videos and studio invention, 'Bush will stake a strong claim to be the female Bowie' (2016: 577). Indeed, an admirer since hearing 'Starman' aged 13, Bush penned a 1973 song in Bowie's honour, 'Humming' (finally released in 2018 on *The Other Side 2*), and attended the final night of Bowie's Ziggy Stardust tour at London's Hammersmith Odeon on 3 July 1973 (Thomson 2015: 18).

Technically, if tendentiously, one could claim that Bush's first film presence comes courtesy of Bowie and his Hammersmith concert which, at the eleventh hour, was preserved for posterity by RCA via D.A. Pennebaker's documentary *Ziggy Stardust and the Spiders From Mars* (1973/1979). Given the venue's poor lighting, Pennebaker encouraged fans to bring along and let off their own camera flashes, a strategy which serves not only to register on Bowie but, with the film cameras regularly switching onto the auditorium, to illuminate each member of the crowd. Thus they share the screen with Bowie, becoming direct participants both in process and end product as Pennebaker works to chart a cultural symbiosis, a mutually enriching double act between the star and his followers. Though not individually discernible, amidst that audience, alongside her brothers and 'only feet from the stage' (Doyle 2022: 42), was Catherine Bush, just shy of her fifteenth birthday, contributing to the audible excitement and the final, teary bemusement as Bowie retired his Ziggy persona.

'Chameleon, comedian, Corinthian and caricature,' Bowie sang in 'The Bewlay Brothers' (1971), and wide-ranging parallels between the two artists would endure. Melodic and vocal inflections weave across Bush's work: reviewing 'The Red Shoes', Stephen Dalton commended how it 'bashes out a jarring cousin of Bowie's "Jean Genie" riff' (*Vox*, October 1993); on 'Heads We're Dancing', Ron Moy finds that 'The whole rhythm section seems to pay tribute to one of pop music's great genre benders – David Bowie' (2007: 109); in 'Sat in Your Lap', Graeme Thomson notes its 'I must admit' section offers 'an astonishingly precise imitation of *Lodger*-period Bowie' and his 'histrionic' singing style (2015: 179); the bridge in 'Breathing', for Christine Kelley, 'sounds like Bowie's similarly cosmic "Space Oddity" in places' (*Dreams of Orgonon*, 19 July 2020).

As with sound, so with vision. Both Bush and Bowie, at different times, studied dance and movement under legendary mime artist Lindsay Kemp (1938–2018): Bush, seeking out her hero's mentor, probably danced to the Bowie numbers Kemp used in his 50p open classes at Covent Garden (Buckley 2005: 51). Extrapolating from this shared training, Moy suggests that, for Bush, '[Bowie's] use of different personae featuring costume changes may have influenced her own subsequent stage performances' (2007: 60). This bringing together of different artforms in a single aim has led to Bowie's approach being labelled 'a kind of *gesamtkunstwerk*' aka a 'total work of art' (Reed 2023: 3–7; Perrott 2024: 4–5). Bush's sole concert tour, retrospectively termed the 'Tour of Life', covering 28 European performances from 2 April to 13 May 1979 in venues ranging from Poole to Paris, justifies comparison to Bowie's concerts, notably his rigidly choreographed 1974 Diamond Dogs tour, with its use of mime and dance during its myriad shifts in costume and characterisation. However, Bush found her touring schedule exhausting – plus, like late-1970s Bowie, spectacularly divisive[4] – and infamously deemed it an experience she would never repeat.

Until, that is, a serendipitous coda. In late-career comebacks, Bowie's *The Next Day* album (8 March 2013), breaking a decade's silence, was paralleled by Bush's surprise 22-date 'Before the Dawn' concert residency (26 August–1 October 2014) at Hammersmith's Eventim Apollo (which sold out in 15 minutes), newly named but the same venue where she saw Bowie perform as Ziggy Stardust.

Nel Dahl observes that:

> People are mystified by Bush's reticence to perform live, but a key reason was her desire to give audiences more than just music. Inspired by the spectacle of David Bowie's *Ziggy Stardust*, she wanted to bring her own cinematic presentation to her performances, and excelled in performing her music as larger-than-life characters.
>
> (2016)

This point is key to the study undertaken here. Alongside the adoption of different personae and the constant quest for artistic development, both artists shared a fixation with the moving image: they were, as Bowie sang on 'Life on Mars?', 'hooked to the silver screen'.[5] However, alongside her refusal to tour, Bush diverged from Bowie in not pursuing a parallel career in feature film straight acting roles, preferring instead to build her new worlds by maximising the potential of and her control over the recording studio and the new medium of the pop video. Here her creations, like Bowie's, have frequently drawn on her love of film and television, most notably for Bush the genres of Gothic horror, science fiction and film noir – and, though often overlooked, comedy.

With his employment of masks, ironic stances and 'forests of quotation marks', Bowie has been regularly defined as 'performing a postmodern persona' (Jeffries 2022: 56–57), and this study advocates a similar apprehension of Kate Bush. The book's practical criticism, seeking through close analysis to explain and evaluate Bush's playful cherry-picking and earnest intertextuality, is underpinned by a theoretical reading of Bush as (predominantly) a postmodern artist. A broad, indeed nebulous, concept loosely equating to (a thoughtful) 'all is permitted' postmodernism manifests itself through mannerism and stylisation, taking from existing objects/images/pronouncements and repeating or realigning them in imitative or ironising juxtapositions. Cultural theorist Fredric Jameson adjudges it a periodising concept, appearing towards the end of the 1970s and correlating new formal features in culture with the emergence of late capitalism, notably communication technologies that facilitate the concerted marketing of style and image in a new global economy (1991: 1–54). As such, it runs chronologically parallel with the emergence of Kate Bush and the development of her distinctive cultural productions both for form and meaning, negotiating new digital technologies such as the Fairlight CMI and CD recording, and international marketing streams such as music video and MTV.

Bush does not, though, fit with Jameson's assessment of postmodernism as producing a 'waning of affect' and a culture of 'flatlessness or depthlessness, a new kind of superficiality in the most literal sense' (1991: 16, 60). Rather than a value-free 'postmodern pop', this study endeavours to demonstrate how Bush's work chimes with Steven Connor's more positive reading of two distinctive (though related) features of the postmodern condition: first, 'its capacity to articulate alternative or plural cultural identities, of groups belonging to the margins of national or dominant cultures'; and second, 'the celebration of the principles of parody, pastiche, stylistic multiplicity and generic mobility' (1989: 186). Bush equates more closely with this interpretation, providing fresh (predominantly but not exclusively female) perspectives on life and art, and yoking together recuperated signifiers that create new lines of enquiry or ironic rethinkings. Within the arts, Connor sees the music industry (like fashion) as particularly conducive to postmodern practice, principally through groups and singers revisiting the *musical* back catalogue (ibid.). Bush, though, like Bowie, expands her sphere of influence beyond music, culling from a wide range of cultural artefacts that intensify the sense of masquerade and performance as she all but disappears into her endlessly mutable creations, 'provoking and confounding the male gaze' (Reynolds and Press 1995: 289) – and protecting her highly valued privacy through the (literally) composed I.

Kate Bush and Academic Study

The comparison between Kate Bush and David Bowie with their postmodern performativity, their crossover stardom and intermedial work does not hold, however, for subsequent research and reputation. Bowie's screen and stage undertakings have latterly generated concerted critical attention (Glynn 2022; Dixon and Black 2022; Reed 2023; Perrott 2024): not so Bush. As a musical and cultural phenomenon Bush has received wide coverage, including (limited) academic exegesis, but the influence of film and television on her work has remained relatively marginalised. There has been a regular release of unauthorised biographies, journalistic works targeted at a general audience that often contain useful primary or summative research, but invariably these only make passing reference to Bush's multimedia endeavours (Jovanovic 2005; Mendelssohn 2010; Thomson 2015; Doyle 2022).[6] The scant book-length academic attention has focused on Bush's record releases and accompanying videos from the perspective of musicology (Moy 2007) or feminist theology/cultural theory (Withers 2010), though the latter provides a chapter-length study of Bush's film and associated album. All these works contain perceptive analysis and are cited in this study, but they do not compete in scope, focus or detail with *Kate Bush and the Moving Image* which, despite the interest shown by my film studies classes, presents (to date) the only full-length, single-authored study devoted to an evaluation of the importance of film and television media to Bush's work in both sound and vision.

Furthermore, while Bowie's more outlandish visual representations have largely found not just exculpation but exaltation, this is not (yet) the case for Bush, whose television and video work, especially in her early years, remains in many quarters the recipient of a scarcely veiled condescension. This study, while not uncritical of artistic excess and overreach, proposes a comprehensive and nuanced counter-argument to the prevailing reductive (and sometimes ridiculing) view of Bush's borrowings from and contributions to the history of pop music and the moving image.

Relevant here is the question of dispassionate critical judgement. While not acceding to the condemnatory appraisal of many (early) reviewers, it is important not to overcorrect and simply adopt, or adapt, the terms of critical discussion from the discourse of the artist under consideration, a distinct possibility when examining Bush and her work. For instance, Bush's film accompaniment to her 1993 album *The Red Shoes*, itself drawing heavily on previous film and fairy-tale versions, creates a work of multi-layered reflexiveness that thereby makes continual references to the conditions of its own functioning: it presents an enclosed conceptual world that can tempt critics to make their own judgements an echo of this self-commentating. Furthermore, as noted, Bush has given articulate and thoughtful explanations for many of her creations, and this study will frequently cite her media pronouncements, taken both from the written (mainstream and music) press and audio-visual media (radio, television and CD interviews). However, while offering alluring themes and terminologies, the (extra) danger is of operating so much within the parameters of Bush's own discourse that the critic fails to provide substantial points of purchase on undoubtedly complex material by bringing it into comprehensible relation with other modes of understanding. Thus, alongside Bush's own interpretations, this study will seek to construct an interpretive framework from a variety of critical observations on intent and from cogent comparisons on achievement, opening up new horizons and different lexicons relevant to enriching an analysis and aiding an appraisal of her use of the moving image.

What is the significance of identifying these borrowings for an appreciation of Bush and her art? To undertake my own first borrowing, film philosopher Noël Carroll identified the cine-literate filmmakers of New Hollywood (1967–1980) as effecting a 'cinema of allusion', where adaptation from pre-exiting visual texts was one aspect of a methodology of voracious borrowings, 'including quotations, the memorialization of past genres, the reworking of classic scenes, shots, plot motifs, lines of dialogue, themes, gestures, and so forth from film history' (1998: 241). I argue in this study that Bush, while always original in her melodies, can be seen as creating, in her lyrics and accompanying visual imagery, a similar 'music of allusion', where pre-existing visual texts have a multi-purpose function as the catalyst to new artworks, a construct to shape emotional display, even a cover to filter personal expression, but also, having divined meanings from her personal experiences, providing a means to render them more comprehensive in scope. Mining these texts enables Bush to achieve an encompassing, postmodern 'pop' aesthetic, blurring distinctions between high and low culture as she borrows from exempla ranging, as this study will show, from the venerated to the vulgar, from a classic pantheon-topping US film like *Citizen Kane* (1941) to a contemporaneous prime-time UK television cop show like *The Sweeney* (1975–1978), in the process creating songs, videos and film work that function as both popular and avant-garde, appealing to multiple audiences of varying ages and education.

This breadth of appeal is vital. If employing allusion is important for artistic production, what is its impact on the resultant work's reception? To borrow again from his study of film, Carroll points out that allusion establishes two tiers of spectatorship – an 'uninformed' level, where spectators simply consume the film in isolation; then an 'informed' level, where spectators recognise how the director has referenced previous films, and thus shares their consciousness of film history. (One could, perhaps, propose a sliding scale to nuance these polarised distinctions.) Carroll notes how most audience members consume allusion-filled films at a surface level, without recognising the allusions. Importantly, however, this should not matter, since the films, if well made, need to work independent of such recognition. The informed spectator, though, passes from consumer to 'connoisseur', and gains a supplementary pleasure from a more cine-literate, intense engagement with the film (1998: 242–248). So too with the music of allusion created by Kate Bush. Her commercial success proves that such a strategy is not intended or understood as exclusive, and certainly not elitist. Her artistic creations function as discrete entities: even so, the allusions they contain can bring an enriching resonance, adding a cultural hinterland to enhance a song and/or its video/film accompaniment.

Nonetheless, having made the above distinction without prejudice, Carroll underlines a resultant and essential symbiosis, how:

> Serious American commercial filmmakers have come to require serious filmgoers – that is, those well enough versed in film history to note references and delicate variations, and sufficiently committed to the pretentions of cinema to bother to decipher such self-conscious gestures – as a prerequisite for anything approaching a full appreciation of their art.
>
> (1998: 245)

This study, aiming to demonstrate a similar symbiosis, is undertaken by a serious listener to the work of a serious musician, and has three broad aims. It evidences the regularity of Bush's recourse to 'self-conscious gestures', that is, her allusions to the visual culture of film and television. The weight of this evidence is in itself significant for 'approaching a full appreciation' of Bush's art, but the second intention is to explore in each instance the reasons for their employment, and the third to analyse their artistic worth, their ability to open out rather than close down different horizons. This investigation hopefully does not make for a dry theoretic discourse: Bush herself often alluded to – and even contributed to – works of comedy, and this study, while committed to the 'pretentions of music', will endeavour not to be overly pretentious in its terminology or thematic explorations.

While informed by the three differing media formats utilised by Bush, the broadly chronological 'set list' for each part of this monograph runs as follows. This introductory chapter, itself tripartite, has explored links with recent streaming series and earlier multimedia artists, before establishing parameters and explaining the methodology at work. It is followed by three sections, each consisting of two chapters. Part 1 explores the visual sourcing of Bush's musical compositions. Within it, Chapter 2 examines how the influence, explicit or implicit, of film and television on Bush's songs is manifest within titles, imagery and narratives across her first six albums. Beginning with her breakthrough hit 'Wuthering Heights' and moving through to 1989's *The Sensual World*, it details the influence of visual media on 20-plus songs, including allusions to works by Walt Disney, Ken Russell, Stanley Kubrick and Francis Ford Coppola. It assesses these songs not as subservient cross-media adaptations but fully reimagined 'parallel texts' with fresh agency and viewpoint. Chapter 3 pauses the chronological taxonomy of moving image influence and examines Bush's bespoke film compositions. These are argued to be far more 'hit and miss' than her more autonomous musical compositions, and cover films by Terry Gilliam, Nicolas Roeg, John Hughes and Chris Weitz. Bush was also active in television, both through bespoke compositions and, uniquely, on-screen. An appraisal is given of her soundtrack work for *The Comic Strip Presents*, while her performance as a 'straight actor' in the 1990 episode *Les Dogs* is shown to demonstrate a charismatic screen presence (sadly) never developed.

Part 2 explores Bush's work within the field of music video. Chapter 4 examines her promo videos directed by third parties, a phase lasting from 1978 to 1985. These are shown to develop swiftly from recorded dance to more ambitiously 'cinematic' pieces, covering state oppression, nuclear war and science-fiction mysticism. A concomitant tension is shown to develop between their artistic expression and the format's commercial expediency. Chapter 5 explores the music videos directed by the more artistically autonomous Bush herself (bar those from *The Red Shoes*, treated separately). All are shown as successfully employing allusion to help create a diegetic structure and provide wider cultural resonance. Investigations of reworked influences range from Alfred Hitchcock to Nigel Kneale, Billy Wilder to David Cronenberg, Lotte Reiniger to Samuel Beckett, supporting a career-wide continuity in performance as personae in unconventional, liminal states, but also demonstrating a maturation from over-determined choreography towards a late physical stillness questioning the very possibilities of visual representation.

Part 3 is devoted to Bush's one sortie into film production. Chapter 6 explores the music of allusion as played out in Bush's seventh album, 1993's *The Red Shoes*, ostensibly her most direct mining of a prior visual text. The album's troubled gestation is outlined, and its press reception explored. The importance of *The Red Shoes* film, and in particular its British director Michael Powell, is summarised, and the album's individual tracks are analysed to show the benefits (or deficiencies) of their internal and wider allusive force. Chapter 7 explores in depth the sole film project of Bush's career, *The Line, The Cross & The Curve* (henceforth *TLTC&TC*). A brief production history explains its genesis and purpose, and how Bush assumed key roles in acting, scriptwriting, choreography and direction. A survey of the (sporadic and lukewarm) press reception follows, before the chapter undertakes a detailed textual analysis – including narrative summaries given the work's inaccessible status. It is shown that, while the paradigm of the red shoes that begins with Hans Christian Andersen is embedded in the film, Bush's production also functions as a microcosm of her creative undertakings, exploring a female-centred mythology where the dancer (re-)finding her identity is not dependent on patriarchal assistance or assent. It is also shown as achieving passages of cinematic accomplishment, working both as a correlative for the music and providing independent visual pleasure. Ultimately, though, the chapter interrogates the perils of allusion: in this longer form, is the cinematic intertextuality sufficiently transmuted into a separate and self-standing art work for it to find a valued position in Bush's oeuvre? A final summative chapter reiterates how, much as her music harnesses modern studio techniques to traditional and instrumental textures, so does Bush harness her lyrics and burgeoning pop video genre to a visual grammar that, while innovative, draws heavily on the western cinematic and televisual canons.

I enter one final counsel before this study continues. *Kate Bush and the Moving Image* is, like my previous books on cross-media pop stars, written from two perspectives: it is authored by both a film/television historian *and* a fan since my own teenage years of Kate Bush and (most of) her works. The historian aims, through precisely referenced contextual and textual analysis, to establish and analyse the importance of the allusions to film and television that run throughout Bush's career. The fan, who may over the years (if daring to apply Carroll's distinctions) have shifted on the scale from consumer to connoisseur, nonetheless seeks to convey the joy, the ambivalence, the challenge, and yes, at times, the disappointment or indeed bemusement experienced in listening to Bush's songs and viewing her video and film productions, always remembering that, beyond any economic imperative, the central purpose of this woman's work has been to share affective and pleasurable audio and visual creations.

Time to explore the 'Strange Phenomena'.

Notes

1 In truth, 'Running Up That Hill' has enjoyed a sustained 'afterlife', notably when a remixed version played over the closing ceremony to London's 2012 Summer Olympics. Other uses include the first episode of *Pose* (FX, tx. 3

June 2018). A 2003 cover version by Placebo has proven particularly popular, featuring inter alia in *Bones* (Fox, series 2, episode 11, 2006), *The Vampire Diaries* (The CW, series 1, episode 1, 2009) and *Big Little Lies* (HBO, series 2, episode 6, 2019). Bush's own live performance of the song (alongside Dave Gilmour) for Amnesty International in March 1987 at the London Palladium also featured in *The Secret Policeman's Third Ball* (Ken O'Neill, 1987).

2 Hence Bush's (commercially unsuccessful) 9 December 1978 performance of 'The Man with the Child in His Eyes' and 'Them Heavy People' on NBC's *Saturday Night Live*.

3 'Strange fascination' is a lyric in David Bowie's 1971 song 'Changes'.

4 Charles Shaar Murray typified the post-punk-era rock press attitude towards Bush, dismissing her London Palladium 'Tour of Life' performance as an 'old-style ideology' betraying 'all the unpleasant aspects of David Bowie in the Mainman era [1972–1975] ... desperate to dazzle and bemuse' (*New Musical Express*, 28 April 1979).

5 Another parallel: both Bush and Bowie, though determined, were frequently self-deprecating regarding their screen performances.

6 Mendelssohn's hybrid volume splices into its biographical study fictional scenes of obsessive Kate Bush fan Lesley Herskovitz.

Part 1
Music

2 It's Like a Film

Kate Bush and Songs Influenced by Screen Media

As with David Bowie, the intrinsic cinematic quality of Kate Bush's music has often been referenced.[1] Biographer Graeme Thomson argues that, outwith any visual accompaniment:

> Her songs are already like little films; they have depth and texture, they create an aural landscape which conjures up clear images, they have shape and proportion, often they have narrative, they carry mood changes, emotions and strong atmosphere. It's all there.
>
> (2015: 280)

Critic Christopher Forrester agrees:

> there is no more revealing or vital component of Bush's work than the inextricable bond between song and moving image; her soundscapes are so dazzling and rich as to allow the ears to possess the eyes and visualize their baroque spectacles as strange ghouls and specters. Individual songs, too, possess a measure of performance that is decidedly cinematic.
>
> (2021)

Bush herself has advocated an inbuilt intermediality:

> when you write a song: the person singing the song is a character. Although it might be you vocally, it's not yourself you are singing about but that character. It's someone who is in a situation, so you treat it like a film. That's how I see songs.
>
> (cited in Diliberto 1990: 72)

The influence, explicit or implicit, of film and television on Bush's work is manifest at the level of titles, images and shaping narratives. In

DOI: 10.4324/9781003479604-3

exploring this aspect, it is important to stress that these sources invariably change shape and significance when filtered through a new creative process. Asked in interview whether she writes songs from fiction out of fear of self-exposure, Bush answered:

> Whenever I base something on a book or a film, I don't take a direct copy. I don't *steal* it. I'll put it through my personal experiences, and in some cases it becomes a very strange mixture of complete fiction and very, very personal fears within me.
>
> (Irwin 1980: 30)

The taxonomy of film and television influences that follows is not undertaken with any intention of impugning Bush's creativity: rather, it shows the power of her artistry in transforming these foundational texts into something unique and personal, a 'strange mixture' that effects significant shifts in emphasis, especially when recalibrated from a different gender perspective.

The influence of the moving image is there from the beginning. 'Wuthering Heights', released through EMI on 20 January 1978 as Bush's debut single and lead release from her first album *The Kick Inside*, became a 'breakout' success, holding number 1 in the UK charts for four weeks, the first time a female artist had topped Britain's charts with a self-penned song. It also reached number 1 in Australia, Ireland, Italy, New Zealand and Portugal as it exceeded 1 million sales for the year. Its success helped lift *The Kick Inside*, released on 17 February, to number 3 on the UK album charts, and to the top spot in Holland and Portugal. Ostensibly literary in inspiration, and indicatively postmodern in working 'to blur, if not totally dissolve, the traditional oppositions and boundaries between the aesthetic and the commercial, between art and the market, and high and low culture' (Shuker 1994: 229), Bush's ghostly power ballad, sung in a high register to signal the singer as howling spirit, was not, however, prompted by reading Emily Brontë's same-named Gothic novel of 1847, but rather when young tv-addict Kate caught the end of BBC2's four-part adaptation (tx. 28 October–18 November 1967). Visually innovative and technologically ambitious in being the novel's first television version with location shooting (Hazette 2015: 188), the BBC's *Wuthering Heights* serial was directed by Peter Sasdy, and starred Angela Scoular as wild and passionate Catherine Linton née Earnshaw and Ian McShane as her tortured soulmate Heathcliff. Bush was captivated in particular by the (genuinely scary) image of Cathy's spectre at the window, pushing her hand bloodily through the glass and whispering to unwanted tenant Lockwood (Jeremy Longhurst) for entry and Heathcliff's forgiveness. A full decade later, having recently read (sections of) Brontë's novel, and employing direct quotes from Cathy – 'Let me in! I'm so cold'; 'bad dreams in the night' – but still with Scoular's impassioned scene uppermost in her imagination, she wrote the song swiftly during the night of 5 March 1977, aged just 18 (*Kate Bush Club Newsletter*, 1, January 1979).

Two promotional videos, choreographed by Bush with input from dance tutor Robin Kovac, were quickly (and cheaply) produced to accompany 'Wuthering Heights'. One version, directed by Nick Abson predominantly for US consumption, places Bush, in a long red dress, out on the 'wiley, windy moors' – actually the MoD's artillery range on Salisbury Plain.[2] An indoor video, directed by future Bush regular Keith MacMillan at Ewart Studios in Wandsworth and targeting the UK/European markets, more fully intimates Cathy as a ghost. Shot in soft focus, it is regularly doubled and brought down generations to create a visual echo effect as Bush, sporting a white chiffon dress, waves, hunches and cartwheels in a dark space while dry ice floats around her feet (Figure 2.1). The week after this version's 2 March 1978 showing on Britain's *Top of the Pops*, 'Wuthering Heights' leapt from fifth place to number 1. Not untypically, both versions, almost

Figure 2.1 'Wuthering Heights' – Window Dressing.

raw in their teenage earnestness and authenticity, have proven enduringly ripe for parody, from (a mocking) Faith Brown (*Faith Brown Chat Show*, ITV, tx. 26 January 1980) to (affectionate) BBC1 Comic Relief performances by Steve Coogan's Alan Partridge (tx. 12 March 1999) and Noel Fielding (tx. 12 March 2011).[3] Nonetheless, Emily Caston sees Bush's first videos as a 'major breakthrough' in redefining the representation of women artists since they 'did not dismember or objectify Bush's body, nor disempower her authorship by editing the footage into sexually-alluring close-ups' (2020: 74).

In addition, I would argue they expand our understanding of wider (canonical) culture. The visual delivery, ghostly yet upbeat, not only modulates the mood of the source text(s) but also, in emphasising the song's first-person narrative, stresses the creation of a different point of view (neither the novel nor the BBC serial inhabits Cathy's consciousness). Thus, Bush's 'Wuthering Heights' can be interpreted as presenting not just a deferential cross-media adaptation but a reimagining or 'parallel text' with Cathy, now granted agency and self-narration, asserting herself as more content than tormented/hysterical, and 'coming home' to Heathcliff after years of purgatory on the moors.[4] Whatever their perceived strengths and weaknesses, both videos draw heavily on the imagery of the BBC adaptation and, an important adjunct to the single's international success, are now generally considered a key pre-MTV contributor to the music video genre.

Bush had to fight to make this her debut single: Bob Mercer and EMI had favoured the more rock-flavoured, if formulaic, track 7, 'James and the Cold Gun' (Mendelssohn 2004: 51). Written years before 'Wuthering Heights', this became a regular number on the KT Bush Band's early pub gigs, and a crowd favourite where Bush would don a cowgirl outfit and mime shooting fellow stage and audience members. While Bush has never ventured a source text, a prevalent view is that the song's (buried) roots go back to the political thriller *The Day of the Jackal* (Fred Zinnemann, 1973), based on Frederick Forsyth's 1971 novel, where Edward Fox's unnamed assassin undertakes the shooting of French President Charles de Gaulle: others infer a reference to Ian Fleming and Eon Productions' licenced-to-kill agent James Bond (Van der Kiste 2021: 24–25). Given the breadth of teenage Bush's film knowledge, both readings are possible, but the most obvious allusion, supported by the song's various theatrical realisations, including her show-closing 'Tour of Life' performances 'with the rear projection screen filled with a classic death valley movie vista' (Thomson 2015: 138), is to the western genre.[5] Given the name addressed and lyrics referencing 'The boys from your gang', one could narrow the focus and propose a female persona and fatalistic narrative derived from *Jesse James* (Henry King, 1939), the recent *The Great Northfield Minnesota Raid* (Philip Kaufman, 1972), or any of the 20-plus films based on legendary American outlaw Jesse Woodson James (1847–1882), leader of the Missouri-based James-Younger gang until his assassination by (the coward) Robert Ford.

Track 4, the soft reggae-styled 'Kite' (released as the B-side to 'Wuthering Heights'), offers both a paean to the transformative powers of dance and a generic narrative of wanderlust leading to the realisation that there's no place like home. If a lyrical source is not obvious, the song became the foundation for the album cover with Bush, spray-painted gold, attached to a giant kite and floating across a giant eyeball. Designed entirely by Bush (again rejecting EMI's preference – for a sexed-up photograph), the inspiration was wholly cinematic, now clearly nodding to Eon's James Bond, specifically Jill Masterson (Shirley Eaton) who, for betraying the titular villain, has her entire body fatally painted in *Goldfinger* (Guy Hamilton, 1964). This was not the primary source, however: album photographer Jay Myrdal has elucidated that the visualisation, extrapolated from the 'Kite' lyrics about a hole in the sky with 'a big eyeball calling to me', came from the (Bush-admired) Disney animation *Pinocchio* (1940) and 'the scene when Jiminy Cricket floats past the whale's eye using his umbrella like a parachute' (*'The Kick Inside* is 40 Years Old Today', *Kate Bush News*, 17 February 2018). The cover thus matches a work where the artist is already skilfully coding her allusions, reshaping them into a unique vision with multivalent address.

From here the influence of the moving image on Bush's songwriting grew apace. Her sophomore album, the rushed-out *Lionheart*, which largely reworked songs from Bush's considerable teenage back-catalogue, was released on 13 November 1978 and peaked at number 6 on the UK chart (her only failure to make the top five). The album may have chosen a title that, like its semi-titular track 5, 'Oh England My Lionheart', evokes an arcadian England, but *Lionheart* is also the title of a 1968 Children's Film Foundation (CFF) movie. Adapted from Alexander Fullerton's 1965 novel and directed by Michael Forlong, it stars the latter's son James Forlong as Andrew Fowler, a boy in Tonbridge who protects a circus-escaped lion (the famed Simba) from a shoot-to-kill army unit including Wilfrid Brambell and pop star Joe Brown. A minor work in the CFF canon, the British Film Institute (BFI)'s periodical termed it 'A rather leisurely children's film whose main attraction is a huge lion, magnificent in appearance but disappointingly (if understandably) lethargic in performance' (*Monthly Film Bulletin*, 36, 426, July 1969: 147). Many critics felt the same about Bush's new release (exhibit A on appearance, the album cover, shot by Gered

Mankowitz, which shows EMI now getting its way by presenting the singer in a tight-fitting lion bodysuit), but the child's-eye perspective and support of the youthful idealism central to CFF films also interweave productively through Bush's album.

This begins with track 2, 'In Search of Peter Pan', which may be musically disjointed but, alongside its mining of J.M. Barrie's cultural icon, develops sonically when Bush, her voice multi-tracked into a choral 'lift off', sings three times 'Second Star on the right / Straight on 'til morning', the directions to the mythical Neverland given to Wendy by Peter in Walt Disney's adaptation of *Peter Pan* (1953). It concludes more ambivalently, though, as she sings, with distorting slowness and in a minor key, the chorus lines from 'When You Wish Upon a Star', the signature song performed in *Pinocchio* by the cover-referenced conscience-character Jiminy Cricket (Cliff Edwards). Childhood, the song's delivery finally seems to admit, is not without its troubles.

The links to cinema (and acknowledgement that adulthood and its greater vicissitudes are inevitable) conclude the album with track 10, 'Hammer Horror'. Released on 27 October 1978 as the album's first single, it only reached number 44 in the UK singles chart but fared better overseas, hitting number 10 in Ireland and 17 in Australia. The song evidently references the British film production company, best known for specialising in the horror genre. However, Bush conceived of the song after viewing *Man of a Thousand Faces* (Joseph Pevney, 1957), a bio-pic – produced by America's Universal-International, not Hammer – starring James Cagney, who played silent movie star Lon Chaney, an actor who, deploying groundbreaking makeup, found fame playing various horror characters. Bush reportedly liked the film's 'Chinese box' nature, with an actor playing an actor playing an actor (*Kate Bush Club Newsletter*, 3, November 1979). The narrative of her song concerns an understudy who, after the original actor is killed in an on-set accident, takes over the lead role of *The Hunchback of Notre Dame* – a role Cagney plays Chaney playing in Universal's film version (Wallace Worsley, 1923). Bush's guilt-ridden narrator ends up haunted by the ghost of the jealous original actor, a colleague and former friend. This is evidently an elaborate postmodern 'construct', but one still open to interpretation as personal experience. The accompanying video shows Bush pursued by a masked assailant (Anthony van Laast, co-choreographer on the 'Tour of Life'), whose hands mimic, surround and finally throttle her (Figure 2.2). Choreographed too broadly to strike as truly sinister, Matthew Lindsay reads the dance denouement as:

Figure 2.2 'Hammer Horror' – Fingers and Thumbs.

thumbing the nose to some of 1978's creepier press coverage; ghoulish predictions and feigned concern, about 'the music biz tightening its grip around her swan-like neck' (*Record Mirror*) and about the 'strange birds gathering in trees' waiting to prey on the 'fragile' Bush (*Sunday Times*).

(2023)

Track 9, the freshly composed 'Coffee Homeground' (released as the B-side to 'Hammer Horror') offers an equally macabre narrative and paranoid/parodic narrator. Performed as a Weimar cabaret pastiche with Kurt Weill-style orchestral scoring and Bush assuming a Lotte Lenya accent and delivery, the singer accuses a host of continually trying to poison her and so refuses all offered drinks. Apparently inspired by a story related to Bush by a US cabbie (Jovanovic 2005: 91), one can still sense cinematic enhancements. Namechecking 'Pictures of Crippin', the wife-poisoning homeopath hanged in Edwardian London, evokes Donald Pleasence's portrayal in *Dr. Crippen* (Robert Lynn, 1963), a film with cinematography by Bush-admired Nicolas Roeg (see Chapter 3). The coffee's 'smell of bitter almonds' and 'your arsenic in the pot of tea' offer a more tonally consistent nod to (the equally overplayed) *Arsenic and Old Lace* (Frank Capra, 1944) where

Cary Grant's child-like but serial murdering spinster aunts Abby and Martha Brewster (Josephine Hull and Jean Adair) again present a darker corrective to blissful notions of never growing up.

Other album tracks, again written years earlier, contain screen references. Track 3, 'Wow', a strong song with a euphoric chorus which, on 5 March 1979, became *Lionheart*'s second single release and (buoyed by the 'Tour of Life') a number 14 UK hit, again discusses the trials of life for an actor (here a gay 'queen' who likes 'hitting the Vaseline'), but this time focuses on failing to make the grade. Bush sings in verse two how he will never be a movie star or 'make *The Sweeney*', referencing the UK police series (ITV, January 1975–December 1978) centred on London's Metropolitan Police's Flying Squad whose nickname was taken from Cockney rhyming slang, 'Sweeney Todd'. It is an apposite reference since the series follows the exploits of Detective Inspector Jack Regan (John Thaw) and his 'bagman' Detective Sergeant George Carter (Dennis Waterman), beyond the reach of Bush's actor as paradigms of 1970s' working-class hypermasculinity (Lamb 2020: 43).

Staying with cop shows and homosexual passion, track 8, 'Kashka from Baghdad', though musically slight, again creates an interesting (if ultimately neutered) narrative, with the inhabitants of a small town wondering at the activities of the titular Iraqi who, rumour runs, lives with another but unknown man – a different type of 'whodunnit'.[6] The source, Bush explained to Ed Stewart:

> came from a very strange American Detective series that I caught a couple of years ago, and there was a musical theme that they kept putting in. And they had an old house, in this particular thing, and it was just a very moody, pretty awful serious thing.
> (*Personal Call*, BBC Radio 1, 1979)

Though never named, a plausible contender would be the US series *Baretta* (ABC, 1975–1978), whose undercover detective Tony Baretta (Robert Blake) resides in a fictional city's rundown King Edward Hotel, and whose theme music, 'Keep Your Eye on the Sparrow', sung over the credits by Sammy Davis Jr., featured regularly during episodes.

Bush's third album, 1980's *Never for Ever*, released in September 1980, became both her first number 1 UK album and the first album by a British female solo artist to top the UK chart. While it seemingly marked Bush's transition from precocious talent to major pop star, her film and television influences (recognisable or recondite) are again foregrounded.

Track 2, 'Delius (Song of Summer)' (the B-side to 'Army Dreamers'), was inspired by British director Ken Russell's television film *Song of Summer*, made for BBC's *Omnibus* programme (tx. 15 September 1968). Adjudged 'one of his best' biographies (Jones 2018: 183) and seen by a precocious 10-year-old Bush – she later termed it 'a beautiful piece of film' (*Paul Gambaccini Radio Programme*, BBC Radio 1, 30 December 1980) – Russell's biopic portrays the last six years in the life of English composer Frederick Delius (1862–1934). During this time Eric Fenby, whose 1936 memoir *Delius as I Knew Him* is the basis for Russell's film, acted as the composer's amanuensis at Grez-sur-Loing, 70 km south of Paris – 'Ta, ta-ta. In b, Fenby', Bush's song declaims. The film's centrepiece offers a poignant contrast to its surrounding enclosed world as a flashback shows Delius (Max Adrian), his eyesight fading, being carried up a mountain in Norway to see the sun for the last time (actually filmed in the Lake District). John Tibbitts notes that, typically, 'Russell makes the most of many opportunities to lend visually imaginative wings to the musical sequences' (2005: 173), and Bush's promo video, directed again by MacMillan and set on a BBC studio-created riverbank, is Russell-like in its flamboyant reimagining and visual concentration. It presents a wheelchair-bound Delius (Paddy Bush) wearing a cardboard sun-mask (a leitmotif in Bush's videography here circumventing accurate physical representation), while Bush lip-synchs as a swan-girl floating on the water, sporting a winged gossamer gown, which she waves in time to the music (Figure 2.3).[7] Outside of Delius' and Russell's direct influences, the garb and gestures of Bush's persona indicate an interest in the iconography and narrative potential of ballet, here Pyotr Tchaikovsky's *Swan Lake* (1877), that would culminate in *The Red Shoes* album and accompanying film.

Track 6, 'The Wedding List', 'another mini-movie, another four-minute psychodrama' (Thomson 2015: 160), tells of a bridegroom Rudi being shot dead on his wedding day, and how the bride takes her revenge, killing the assailant then taking her own life. Though possessing a jaunty up-tempo melody and inflected with a dark humour, the number was strongly influenced by François Truffaut's elegant Golden Globe-nominated revenge drama *The Bride Wore Black / La Mariée était en Noir* (1968) – 'an amazing film' Bush enthused (Irwin 1980: 29) – itself based on the same-named 1940 noir novel by Cornell Woolrich. In Truffaut's most direct homage to Hitchcock (his film includes several allusions to 1964's *Marnie*), the newly married groom is accidentally murdered on the church steps by a five-man hunting party horsing around with a loaded rifle in a hotel room across the

Figure 2.3 'Delius (Song of Summer)' – Bush's Swan Song.

street. Jeanne Moreau's widowed bride Julie Kohler (*colère* = anger) vows vengeance on Delvaux (Daniel Boulanger), the man who fired the fatal bullet: after ruthlessly murdering his four friends, she allows herself to be arrested so she can kill the currently incarcerated Delvaux. A staged performance of the song on the *Kate Bush Christmas Special* aka *Kate* (BBC1, tx. 28 December 1979), derived from her 'Tour of Life' and overly melodramatic in delivery for the small screen even if mostly played for laughs, may have a Wild West decor and a crazed Bush in bridal dress gurning and gunning down her saloon-bar bandit nemesis (Paddy Bush), but it still renders explicit the narrative linkage – though not Truffaut's Renoir-like lightness of touch nor Moreau's more reserved and 'highly ambiguous' central protagonist (Holmes and Ingram 1998: 99).

In Bush's defence, the transposition of a source text's moral ambiguity was tackled directly on track 8, 'The Infant Kiss'. This spartan haunting lullaby relates the first-person confessions of a conflicted governess, troubled by the affection she feels when passionately kissed on the lips by her young male charge, possessed, she believes, by the spirit of an adult.[8] The song is directly inspired by Jack Clayton's revered psychological horror film *The Innocents* (1961), itself adapted from *The Turn of the Screw*, Henry James' 1898 Gothic ghost novella.

Clayton's adaptation, scripted by William Archibald and Truman Capote, follows Miss Giddens (Deborah Kerr), the new governess for orphaned siblings Miles (Martin Stephens) and Flora (Pamela Franklin) at a country estate: she becomes convinced her angel-faced charges are possessed by the spirits of violent valet Peter Quint (Peter Wyngarde) and previous governess Mary Jessel (Clytie Jessop), lovers who recently died in the house. Lauded by Neil Sinyard as a cinematic 'pearl of ambiguity', one can read the children as indeed possessed, or equally as the neurotic – and ultimately fatal – projections of a sexually repressed Victorian spinster (2000: 81, 92). Of additional interest to a musician introducing the Fairlight sampler to her compositions, the film's creeping horror was, alongside Georges Auric's orchestral score, sporadically conveyed by the pioneering synthesised sounds created by Daphne Oram, co-founder in 1958 of the BBC Radiophonic Workshop. Bush's song, though differently textured with minimalist string (viol and lirone) accompaniment and fretful vocal, conveys a similar sense of horror both in place and person. With echoes of 'Wuthering Heights' in prioritising the female perspective, Thomson also sees it as a 'daring' take on Bush's world view: 'how often she sings of love and sexual desire as a form of possession, a taboo, a terrifying and unwanted ghost-demon stealing into our heart and bones' (2015: 173). This time, however, Bush was at pains to clarify in interviews that, despite lyrics admitting never to have become enamoured of 'A little boy' before, the song was not a study in paedophilia. Rather, as Tom Doyle notes, she conveys her protagonist as 'terrified by her confused sexual feelings – and what others might think if they knew about them – and absolutely not revelling in them' (2022: 121). It is a musical construct that does not betray the source film's unsettling complexity.

Bush's fourth album, *The Dreaming*, produced by Bush herself and released on 13 September 1982, has been adjudged, according to taste, either a sonic breakthrough or an unhinged artistic dissipation – Bush herself, noting journalistic responses, termed it her 'she's gone mad album' (Phil Sutcliffe, 'Iron Maiden', *Q*, 38, November 1989).[9] Though termed uncommercial, it still reached number 3 in the UK album chart, and became her first US Billboard 200 entry, peaking at 157. Bush stated in interview with John Shearlaw that she wanted to go 'all the way', to be 'experimental and quite cinematic' ('The Shock of the New', *Record Mirror*, 11 July 1981), and the album is again replete with film references, though now mostly reworking/absorbing themes and settings rather than direct quotation. For instance, track 6's titular 'The Dreaming' (reaching number 48 in the UK when released as lead single on 26 July 1982), tells of the destruction of Aboriginals' sacred grounds by white Australians mining for weapons-grade uranium. Though not a direct influence, Matt Lindsay (cogently) argues that the song 'elicits comparisons with Nic Roeg's *Walkabout* (1971), not just due to its setting but in its tragic understanding of the human inability to communicate (a recurrent Bush theme)' (2012). Track 7, 'Night of the Swallow', may concern smuggling and have a musical framework stamped Ireland (where it was released in September 1982 as a (non-charting) single), but Paul Simper hears (perhaps less persuasively) a film noir influence:

> the female is straight out of the awesome Barbara Stanwyck mould of *Double Indemnity* [Billy Wilder, 1944]. She's a domineering, passionate woman who not only doesn't want her lover to risk his life trafficking refugees because of the danger to him, but because she wants him.
>
> ('Dreamtime is Over', *Melody Maker*, 16 October 1982)

Track 9, 'Houdini', is evidently based on the life (and death) of famed Budapest-born escapologist (and occasional silent film actor) Erich Weisz aka Harry Houdini (1874–1926). Houdini was also a believer in spiritualism who spent years debunking fraudsters, and Bush's composition, sung from the viewpoint of his wife and stage assistant Bess, dwells on the code phrase the couple agreed – 'Rosabel, believe' – so they would know that any communication from beyond the grave was genuine. During his career, Houdini's most famous trick was the Chinese Water Torture Cell where, feet locked in stocks, he was lowered upside down into a water-filled tank. In the song Bess explains a regular means of escape from this and other challenges, by passing the key with a kiss. Bush clearly relished the image, re-enacting the key exchange (in sepia) on the album cover with real-life partner and bassist/sound engineer Del Palmer playing her Houdini.[10] So far, so true to the escapologist's received biography (Kalush and Sloman 2006). However, Houdini died of peritonitis and not, as in the song, when the Water Torture trick goes wrong and he is brought out too late. This far more dramatic exit indicates the influence on Bush's composition of Paramount's biopic *Houdini* (George Marshall, 1953) starring Tony Curtis as Harry and Janet Leigh as Bess, which also ends with this (considerable) artistic licence.

'Suspended in Gaffa', track 4 and, from 2 November 1982, the third single release in Europe then Australia, contains no reference to a specific film, but Christine Kelley notes how its 'nature of aporia ... is cinematic' (*Dreams of Orgonon*, 14 September 2020). Beyond this, the titular heavy-cotton black gaffa tape is regularly employed in film and stage productions (reputedly named after the 'gaffer', chief lighting technician on a film crew); film effects are cited as 'it all goes slow-mo'; the song even flirts with Lacanian theory, popular with early-1970s film writers such as Christian Metz and Laura Mulvey, when Bush sings self-reflectively about 'That girl in the mirror'.

More explicit in its film allusions, track 2, 'There Goes a Tenner', a slight and affected ballad, became the album's third – and quasi-novelty – single in Britain (released 2 November 1982) but her poorest-ever commercial endeavour, only reaching number 93. The song draws on old heist films, but while its protagonists ape Hollywood stars, comparing themselves to Humphrey Bogart, James Cagney, George Raft and Edward G. Robinson, they show themselves to be more like Ealing amateurs – one could cite *The Lavender Hill Mob* (Charles Crichton, 1951) and *The Ladykillers* (Alexander Mackendrick, 1955) – as the lyrics recount their bungled bank robbery. Explaining her desire to oppose generic conventions, Bush cited *Butch Cassidy and the Sundance Kid* (George Roy Hill, 1969) as instancing how Hollywood troublingly seeks to 'glorify' such events: 'they always make the robbery something very heroic and fun' (*The Dreaming* Interview Picture Disc, 1982). It is, for once, not a secure choice. The film's memorable pairing of Robert Redford and Paul Newman as the glamorous titular outlaws, the witty screenplay from William Goldman and jaunty Burt Bacharach score all support Bush's premise, but her example is problematised since this self-conscious revisionist western is simultaneously set on 'gently sending up the mythology of the western outlaw' (Turner 1999: 193), as when Butch and Sundance's over-zealous hold-up of the Union Pacific Overland Flyer sends money exploding into the air, an exact parallel for the avowedly unheroic narrative climax that names Bush's song. Nonetheless, the video, directed by Paul Henry – which adds to the mix an arbitrary touch of *The Cabinet of Dr. Caligari / Das Cabinet des Dr. Caligari* (Robert Wiene, 1920) with its skewed set and low-key lighting – can be viewed, given its female vocals and images of a nervous Bush and gang (including regular dance partner Gary Hurst) in dark jumpsuits (Figure 2.4), as offering a corrective to the heist genre's endemic (white) hypermasculine cool and competence. Against that, the work's postmodern drive towards de-differentiation, the breaking down of social divisions, does not here extend to class. Given Bush's upper-bourgeois home counties upbringing, the song's pantomimic 'cock-er-nee' vocal impressions are not immune from accusations of class condescension. However read, 'There Goes a Tenner' has to be adjudged a concatenation of precarious ideas and, like its protagonists, ultimately unsuccessful.

Figure 2.4 'There Goes a Tenner' – Bush Goes to Ealing.

In an album of myriad voices, track 3, 'Pull Out the Pin', at first languid then livid/desperate in (double-tracked) delivery as it relates how a North Vietnamese soldier pursues his American prey day and night, had a more direct visual inspiration. Although the operatic and hallucinogenic behemoth *Apocalypse Now* (Francis Ford Coppola, 1979) was still culturally resonating, the song, Bush informed her fanbase, was instead prompted by seeing on television a short and unflinching Australian documentary that gave a rare Vietcong perspective. Though not named by Bush, this will have been the Academy Award-nominated *Front Line* (David Bradbury, 1979), a 55-minute profile of Tasmanian-born combat news-cameraman Neil Davis who spent 11 years filming in the Vietnam combat zone. Bush elaborated how, following the documentary, her song was created in purely cinematic terms:

> We sat in front of the speakers trying to focus on the picture – a green forest, humid and pulsating with life. We are looking at the Americans from the Vietnamese point of view and, almost like a camera, we start in wide shot. Right in the distance you can see the trees moving, smoke and sounds drifting our way … sounds like a radio. Closer in with the camera, and you can catch glimpses of their pink skin … Take the camera in even closer, and we find a solitary soldier, perhaps the one I have singled out … I move

towards the sleeping man. A helicopter soars overhead, he wakes up, and as he looks me in the eyes I relate to him as I would to a helpless stranger ... The moving pictures freeze-frame and fade – someone stopped the multi-track, there's more overdubs to do.

(*Kate Bush Club Newsletter*, 12, October 1982)

The resultant underrated composition (with Pink Floyd's Dave Gilmour adding calmly threatening backing vocals) is, unlike its predecessor, an achieved number, rendering an oppressive cinematic sensuality, a synaesthetic heart of darkness.

The album closer, track 10, 'Get Out of My House', has been read as a personal commentary from Bush on the invasive nature of fame (Thomson 2015: 191): if so, it is again refracted through the postmodern construct of cinematic allusion. The song's start, and particularly its ending, where Bush assumes the character of a frantically braying mule ('Hee-Haw / Hee-Haw') has provoked derisive laughter and/or the reaction that 'you've totally lost it, girl' (Doyle 2022: 147), but it draws again on Disney's *Pinocchio*, specifically the visit to cursed Pleasure Island where errant young Lampwick (Frankie Darro), because of his misdeeds, is transformed into a donkey. Bush termed this 'an incredibly heavy scene' (Doug Alan, *Interview*, January 1986, https://gaffa.org/dreaming/doug_int.html), while for film critic Leonard Maltin (and my infant self) it 'ranks among the most terrifying moments in screen history' (1987: 59). The singer's initial transformation ('I turn into a bird') can again recall (less frightening) Disney, namely the practical education effectuated by the wizard Merlin with young Arthur aka Wart in *The Sword in the Stone* (1963), adapted from T.H. White's 1938 novel – Wart at one point is changed into a sparrow so he can learn how to fly, a helpful skill if needing to escape.

In a more totalising influence on 'Get Out of My House', Bush pointed fans towards the fear and isolation portrayed in *Alien* (Ridley Scott, 1979), and especially Stephen King's 1977 novel *The Shining* and its film adaptation (Stanley Kubrick, 1980) (*Kate Bush Club Newsletter*, 12, October 1982). The song here merits analysis as an effective paradigm for Bush's compositional techniques since, while alluding to characters and incidents from Kubrick's film, she transforms its cool (and masculinist) precision to fit her distinctive Gothic (and female-centred) sensibility in a tale of lovelorn retreat. Noël Carroll, in his seminal study of cinema's allusive propensities, felt that Kubrick's *The Shining* was too skewed towards allusion to function independently at a surface, consumer level (1998: 248). It is a debatable judgement, but is less applicable to Bush's song where, even without a knowledge of source texts, the song coheres as describing a woman retreating after the break-up of a relationship, struggling but determined to stay strong. The lyrics where she terms herself a concierge barring all entry to her home can be read as referencing an internal watchdog, the protagonist protesting that someone (or something – past memories? Burgeoning insanity?) will not broach her (emotional) lockdown. Knowing the Kubrick source, however, adds another 'informed' level of reception, evoking *The Shining*'s aspiring writer and recovering alcoholic Jack Torrance (Jack Nicholson) who is working as off-season caretaker at the Overlook Hotel in the isolated Colorado Rockies. This recognition continues as Bush alludes to the film's blood-filled elevator descending, before the number concludes with the additional imagery of animal transformation, the protagonist remaining stubbornly defiant, or retaliatory (or unhinged) like a braying mule. If King's book had stressed Jack's alcoholism, the film version, with Jack's descent into violence, shifts the focus towards the potential for domestic abuse (Hornbeck 2017: 689–719). A connoisseur's cinephilic reading reveals another potential cause for the narrator's isolation in Bush's song: here, vulnerable and terrified to let anyone in, is a newly affective rendition of *The Shining*, a parallel text that, signalled by the gender role shift for the concierge, frames things from the previously marginalised perspective of Jack's wife, the abused Wendy Torrance (Shelley Duvall).[11] As with 'Wuthering Heights', here is an accomplished artistic expansion of a canonical work.

By the end of *The Shining*, axe-wielding Jack has become the predatory Big Bad Wolf from James Halliwell-Phillipps' version of the 'Three Little Pigs' fairy tale, threatening his family that 'I'll huff and I'll puff and I'll blow your house in!' Bush would deploy related animal imagery, again (though more benignly) treating the fear of emotional attachment, on the title track to her fifth album, *Hounds of Love*, released on 16 September 1985. The album was an important critical and commercial success: nominated for Best British Album at the 1986 Brit Awards, it became her second chart topper in the UK and reached number 30 on the Billboard 200. Hugely successful across Europe, it ranks as her best-selling studio album to date, with over 1 million sales ('100 Greatest Albums Ever', *Q*, 137, February 1998).[12]

Though 'Hounds of Love', track 2 and the album's third single release (on 24 February 1986), hit a modest number 18 in the UK chart, it reached more deeply into film history. It opens with 'It's in the trees! It's coming', a sampled line from Jacques Tourneur's *Night of the Demon* (1957), spoken by Maurice Denham's accursed Professor Harrington. It is more fully informed, though, by the director-producers of her beloved *The Red Shoes* through their adaptation of Mary Webb's 1917 novel *Gone to Earth* (Powell and Pressburger, 1950) – or, more accurately, *The Wild Heart* (1952), the radically reworked version pushed by American producer David O. Selznick, and the print then commonly aired on television.[13] The song's lines on cradling 'a fox caught by dogs' can be confidently linked to 'child of nature' Hazel Woodus (Jennifer Jones) and her relationship with the tame cub Foxy she hides from the hunt. The animal serves as a metaphor for her own predicament, hounded ultimately to her doom by the differing attentions of local squire Jack Reddin (David Farrar) and pastor Edward Marston (Cyril Cusack). (For the accompanying video's further cinematic freight, see Chapter 3). Again, though, the personal reading remains: behind all the allusion, Ian Cawood argues that, in a male-led music industry, the number 'subtly reflects Bush's own public persona' and her determination to 'carve out a uniquely female … voice' (2006: 46).

Track 4, 'Mother Stands for Comfort', is an eerie lullaby where the cold musical texture of synthesisers and drum machines matches the singer's distinct lack of feeling. This is ostensibly about the mother of a murderer, ready to protect her son at all costs. However, the dislocation in a chorus that declares how 'Mother hides the madman' and 'will stay mum', plus the verse admission of being possessed by fear that breaks free of its cage to 'Make me do this', take us away from maternal self-sacrifice and into the domain of split personality disorder. This study of a male murderer, the softly repeated 'mother', plus the extended avian imagery (Kuhn 1994: 94–95), replay another Hitchcock film much admired by Bush, the horror classic *Psycho* (1960), based on Robert Block's same-named 1959 novel, where we discover that secluded motel proprietor (and slasher movie progenitor) Norman Bates (Anthony Perkins), in addition to his penchant for stabbing guests and stuffing birds, has assumed the identity of the mother he jealously killed alongside her lover ten years earlier.

The second side of *Hounds of Love* is taken up by 'The Ninth Wave', a suite comprising seven linked tracks, where the narrative voice, adrift at sea after falling from a ship, hopes for rescue (which finally arrives), but is meanwhile prey to the darker workings of her imagination. The suite takes its name both from lines in Alfred, Lord Tennyson's 1859 'The Coming of Arthur', the first part of his poem cycle *Idylls of the King* (and quoted in the album liner notes), and from the 1850 painting of a shipwrecked group clinging to debris, also called 'The Ninth Wave', by Russian-Armenian marine artist Ivan Aivazovsky. The premise is reminiscent of William Golding's 1956 novel *Pincher Martin* whose titular lieutenant struggles to survive when his warship sinks in the North Atlantic, though in interview Bush offered that:

It's hard to say where it came from. I can only pinpoint certain war films as imagery that would suggest it, things like *The Cruel Sea* [Charles Frend, 1953], those kind of old war films, where the people were being cast into the water, having really been through kind of a heavy experience already.

(*The Dreaming* Interview Picture Disc, 1982)

Similarly, rather than poetry, painting or prose, Bush later emphasised to Richard Skinner how, 'From the beginning, 'The Ninth Wave' was a *film*, that's how I thought of it' ('Classic Albums Interview: *Hounds of Love*', BBC Radio 1, 26 January 1992), and amidst the suite's cinematic unfolding, switching scenes and time frames as the singer's drifting consciousness slowly succumbs to the waves, discrete film elements come to the surface. The third track, the busy polyphonic 'Waking the Witch', has echoes of *Witchfinder General* (Michael Reeves, 1968) as, plunging listeners into the realm of folk horror, again with a distaff perspective, the singer relives a medieval trial where, though innocent, she is persecuted by a witch-hunter and his jury, pushing her underwater to see if she will sink or swim. The next track, 'Watching You Without Me', where the floating woman imagines current events in her home, reminds Graeme Thomson of Dickens' *A Christmas Carol* (1843), arguably best realised for screen in *Scrooge* (Basil Desmond Hurst, 1951), as the singer 'gazes unseen at her own life … invisible, cut off and powerless to communicate (2015: 208). More directly, on the suite's penultimate track, 'Hello Earth', the choral section to this planetary lullaby, performed by the Richard Hickox Singers, is taken from the Georgian folk song 'Zinzkaro' ('By The Spring'), which Bush first heard the Vocal Ensemble Gordela singing on the soundtrack to Werner Herzog's *Nosferatu the Vampyre / Nosferatu Phantom der Nacht* (1979).

Bush's next album, *The Sensual World*, released on 16 October 1989, reached number 2 on the UK chart and became her best-selling album to date in the United States, reaching number 43 and eventually clocking up 500,000 sales. Film links again circulate. Track 7, 'Between a Man and a Woman', which questions the benefits of third-party involvement with a couple's difficulties, may be musically underwhelming and lyrically on-the-nose ('Stay out of this / This isn't your problem'), but it took its title, as Bush told Len Brown, from a line in *The Godfather* (Francis Ford Coppola, 1972), 'during some family argument when Marlon Brando says, "Don't interfere: it's between a man and a woman"' ('In the Realm of the Senses', *New Musical Express*, 7 October 1989). Indicative of Bush's cinephilia, she is referencing here a deleted scene (only included with the 1981 *Godfather Epic* boxed-set). When Don Vito Corleone (Brando) is in a meeting (discussing the film industry) with eldest son Santino aka Sonny (James Caan) and family consigliore Tom Hagen (Robert Duvall), Vito's daughter Connie (Talia Shire) rushes downstairs crying, whereupon Sonny threatens to admonish his sister's husband, Carlo Rizzi (Gianni Russo). Vito interjects: 'sit down, sit down, you never interfere between a man and a woman'. It is an intriguing trigger for Bush, since Vito's edict, despite the evident mistreatment of his daughter, delineates the unyielding conservative gender dynamics of Sicilian family life and, one could argue, of *The Godfather* itself with its machoistic worldview that 'relates to women in a variety of pathological ways' (Camon 2000: 67).

Against this offshoot from an insistently patriarchal source text, *The Sensual World* concluded with the female advocacy and emotional punch of track 10, 'This Woman's Work'. Given that the number was commissioned for a feature film, this marks a useful point to pause the taxonomy of moving image influence on Bush's songs and examine, in Chapter 3, her bespoke film and television compositions.

Notes

1 'It's like a film' is a line from Bush's ca. 1977 demo 'Scares Me Silly' aka 'Really Gets Me Going', available on bootleg CDs. This and other chapter headings crave indulgence for borrowing from Bush's song titles/lyrics.
2 This 'red dress' version inspired 'The Most Wuthering Heights Day Ever', a flash mob event started by Brighton-based art group Shambush in 2013, and now an annual global happening, held in July to coincide with Bush's birthday; 2023 saw 33 such events around the world (Ciara O'Loughlin, '500 Kate Bush Fans at Sydney Park', *Daily Mail*, 15 July 2023).
3 Comedian/impressionist Faith Brown accompanied her parody by describing Bush's early performances as 'choreography for the deaf' (*Faith Brown Chat Show*, 26 January 1980). Far from offended, Bush reputedly wrote Brown a four-page letter of appreciation (Mendelsohn 2004: 53).
4 As such, Bush's song and videos function towards Emily Brontë's text much as Jean Rhys'1966 novel *Wide Sargasso Sea* functions towards sister Charlotte's *Jane Eyre* (also 1847), privileging a character previously denied self-expression (here Rochester's first wife Bertha aka 'the madwoman in the attic').
5 A live (6.25-minute) version of 'James and the Cold Gun' was eventually released on 3 September 1979 as part of the EP *Kate Bush Live on Stage*, recorded at the May 13 Hammersmith Odeon concert.
6 Though exoticised and deprived of agency, the most liberating aspect of this depiction of gay love was Bush electing to perform it on the children's television programme *Ask Aspel* (BBC 1, tx. 5 September 1978).
7 Alongside the video's airing on *The Russell Harty Show* (BBC1, tx. 25 November 1980), Bush was interviewed with an aged (and uncomprehending)

Fenby. Later musicians were more attuned: Simon Reynolds advances that 'the frou-frou side of Cocteau Twins could be traced to a single song on *Never for Ever*, "Delius (Song of Summer)"' ('Kate Bush, the queen of art-pop who defied her critics', *Guardian*, 21 August 2014).

8 'Un Baiser d'Enfant', a version with French lyrics by François Cahan, was released in June 1983 on the Canadian/US mini-LP *Kate Bush* and B-side to the Canada/France-released single 'Ne T'Enfuis Pas'.

9 Another David Bowie link: Tony Visconti, who wrote to Bush a *Lionheart*-inspired fan letter while producing Bowie's *Lodger* album, was briefly considered as producer for *The Dreaming* (Thomson 2015: 178–179).

10 The image also impressed Dua Lipa, whose November 2023 hit 'Houdini' recalls Bush with its key-in-mouth promo artwork.

11 Duvall's on-set mistreatment by Kubrick is now known to have doubled that of Wendy by Jack (Oliver 2020: 215), thus presenting a less palatable 'Chinese box' nature than Bush had admired with *Man of a Thousand Faces*.

12 *Hounds of Love* was employed as the title for Ben Young's 2016 psychological crime film, ostensibly to evoke its 1980s setting.

13 The Powell-Pressburger version would eventually re-establish itself after a heralded BFI restoration in 1985.

3 Be Kind to My Mistakes
Kate Bush and Bespoke Soundtrack Work

Like David Bowie, not the least of Kate Bush's talents was her ability to select skilled individuals and their entourage to work with. In music there was, inter alia, her mentor Dave Gilmour, brother Paddy, and partner Del Palmer: so too in her visual work, with mentorship from Terry Gilliam, and direction, acting turns and creative contributions from Peter Richardson and fellow young comedians. Nonetheless, unlike the near-unfaltering success, indeed sanctification, of her single and album releases, Bush's bespoke contributions to and compositions for film and television, analysed in this chapter, can be considered far more 'hit and miss' in result and reputation.

The start was inauspicious. As an entry to film music, Bush was reputedly invited to record the slow ballad written by John Barry and Hal David for their next commission, but she declined. Explanations range from lack of time in her schedule to the song not suiting her, so Shirley Bassey stepped forward to perform the opening theme to Eon Productions' eleventh James Bond juggernaut, the spy-in-space Roger Moore-starring *Moonraker* (Lewis Gilbert, 1979) (Mendelssohn 2004: 98; Thomson 2015: 124). Instead of 'Moonraker', Bush chose to record 'Magician', written by Maurice Jarre with lyrics by Paul Webster, and a song now all but forgotten. Recorded in February 1979 – a break for Bush from the stressful build-up to her April 'Tour of Life' – and supported by the London Symphony Orchestra, the number featured in Cannon Films' *The Magician of Lublin* (Menahem Golan, 1979), adapted from Isaac Bashevis Singer's 1960 novel, and starring Alan Arkin as Yasha Mazur, the eponymous late-nineteenth-century Jewish conjurer and conman who tours Eastern Europe and wants to learn how to fly. Sprinkled with gestures to mysticism akin to Bush's own work – Mazur finally turning into a flying goose (sic) was an image she would remember (see Chapter 4) – the film proved (unlike *Moonraker*) a box-office and critical disaster: Tim Pulleine typically bemoaned how, with its 'shopworn behavioural shorthand' and 'cliched syntax', 'the movie's imaginative world remains perfunctory in the extreme' (*Monthly Film Bulletin*, 47, 552, January 1980, 49). Even Bush's supposedly titular contribution is employed as an underscore, its lyrics at times barely audible beneath the equally stilted dialogue. This fairground-inflected waltz, never commercially released, at least registers as Bush's first turn as the original performer of another's composition.

'Magician' also made it onto the finished film, unlike Bush's next cinema foray. In 1984, American composer Michael Kamen (best known for scoring Pink Floyd's 1979 album *The Wall*) was entrusted by Embassy International Pictures to score Terry Gilliam's *Brazil* (1985), another study of a man desperate to take flight, and a work regarded as quintessentially postmodern by dint of its 'parodic references to other movies' and 'co-existence of heterogeneous filmic genres' (Hutcheon 1988: 5). As a leitmotif for Gilliam's comedy-sci-fi dystopia, registering scenes where Sam Lowry (Jonathan Pryce)'s lowly bureaucrat at the Ministry of Information dreams of a paradisical elsewhere where he is a heroic winged warrior swooping through the air to find his ideal woman, Kamen employed variations of Ary Barroso's 1939 song 'Brazil' ('Aquarela do Brasil'), ranging from lush string instrumentals to performances by American folk-blues singer Geoff Muldaur. Working to create a sense of Walter Mitty meeting Franz Kafka, Peter Marks notes how 'that song underscores how *Brazil* depicts less a place than a state of mind, an attitude, a utopian destination, and a potentially rebellious cry against repressive authority' (2009: 91). Bush was a great admirer of Gilliam's work, back to his cartoon animations for *Monty Python's Flying Circus* (BBC, 1969–1974), and willingly recorded a further version of 'Brazil'. This rendition, however, did not make the final film cut or the original soundtrack release. No official explanation has been offered, though Bush's distinct vocal version was perhaps tonally askew, both too foregrounded and elegiac compared with the variants scored elsewhere. Perhaps it suffered due to the film's shift in gender focus, as Gilliam's dissatisfaction with the acting performance of relative newcomer Kim Griest led to the role of Lowry's 'dream girl' Jill Layton being reduced and reconstructed until 'she becomes more a catalyst for Sam's actions than the active agent Gilliam had planned' (Marks 2009: 92). Whatever the cause, Bush's version, complete with its postmodern summation that 'Tomorrow was another day', has appeared as 'Sam Lowry's First Dream (Brazil)' on re-releases of the film soundtrack.

A more successful commission followed in February 1987 when Bush wrote and recorded 'Be Kind to My Mistakes', a song that plays over the opening title sequence of Cannon Screen Entertainment's *Castaway* (Nicolas Roeg, 1986) and equally opens its soundtrack album.[1] Roeg's film, another vision of escaping mundane reality, was adapted from Lucy Irvine's same-named 1984 memoir, and relates her experiences after answering an offer in *Time Out* magazine's small ads section to spend a year on a deserted island (Tuin in the Torres Strait) with writer Gerald Kingsland. 'Be kind to my mistakes' are the words spoken by Kingsland (Oliver Reed) at the film's conclusion, concerned at what Irvine will write about their time together. Otherwise comprising an instrumental score by Stanley Myers, Neil Sinyard stresses that the film does 'take cognizance of Kingsland's counter-version of events in his book, *The Islander* [also 1984]' (1991: 105), a point (of view) emphasised by beginning with Bush's number which, with an effective structural symmetry, is finally revealed as Kingsland's earnest request. Amanda Donohoe played Irvine, though rumours persist that Bush's contribution resulted from director Roeg first attempting to cast her in the role – she again passed, either baulking at spending months on an isolated shoot with the drunken Reed, or because of the expected nude scenes (Mendelssohn 2004: 210; Thomson 2015: 278).

Bush's most achieved film commission came in March 1987 when she recorded 'This Woman's Work' at the behest of producer-director John Hughes for his romantic comedy *She's Having a Baby* (1988). The song, reflecting on the act of childbirth from a male perspective, was written expressly to be used during the previously lightweight film's tonal-shift climax when, waiting in hospital, Jake Briggs (Kevin Bacon) is informed that the breech labour of his wife Kristy (Elizabeth McGovern) is endangering both her life and their child's. As the song plays, a flashback montage intercuts a reflective Jake (and medical instruments being selected in the operating theatre) with treasured moments from the couple's earlier years, walking down the aisle, incompetently decorating their new home, getting caught in the rain, and kissing. It is the film's key scene, which, as Bush sings how 'the craft of the father' starts here, portrays Jake, suddenly deprived of agency, realising 'the dizzying responsibility of parenthood' and, like many Hughes protagonists, facing 'the dawning pitfalls and accountabilities that are inevitable in the process of growing into adulthood' (Christie 2012: 169). Composed while Bush viewed the completed scene, the music dovetails with the action in breadth and detail, as when the line 'Give me your little kiss' matches the memory of the couple sharing a brief hallway kiss (Figure 3.1). Alongside the sequence's emotive acting and montage technique, Bush's contribution, sung to piano and Fairlight accompaniment, skilfully delivers this potentially jarring passage to maturity.

Figure 3.1 She's Having a Baby – 'It's Hard on the Man' (Discuss).

Originally released on the film's soundtrack album, a year later, re-edited with orchestral overdubs, it was included on – and fits with the themes of – Bush's next studio album, *The Sensual World* (1989). Selected as the album's second single release (with 'Be Kind to My Mistakes' as the B-side), it reached number 25 in the UK charts and, alongside proving a perennial fan-favourite, has grown from its bespoke origins to become one of Bush's most frequently covered and soundtracked compositions.[2]

Bush's work for Roeg and Hughes was bracketed with less successful ventures. In 1999 she wrote 'Out of the Storm' for *Dinosaur* (Eric Leighton, 2000), Disney's first all-digital feature film. The commissioned number was intended to enhance a poignant scene where the animated characters look back at their destroyed Lemur Island. As with *Brazil*, however, the song ultimately failed to make the soundtrack. It seems that, with preview audiences responding unfavourably to Bush's (overly upsetting? Internationally incomprehensible?) lyrics, Disney proposed it be rewritten as an instrumental piece: Bush declined, and the number was dropped (Mendelssohn 2004: 270–271). All was not lost, though. Bush eventually reworked the song for a new commission: it became 'Lyra' which, now referencing lead character Lyra Belacqua (Dakota Blue Richards) and her coming of age, played over the closing credits to New Line's *The Golden Compass* (Chris Weitz, 2007), a fantasy adventure adapted from 1995's *Northern Lights*, the first in (Bush's friend) Philip Pullman's *Dark Materials* novel trilogy. While the film drew muted reviews – James Christopher indicatively praised the 'marvellous' special effects, but bemoaned a 'lack of genuine drama' and how 'the books weave a magic the film simply cannot match' (*Times*, 27 November 2007) – Bush's mournful contribution, accompanied by Oxford's Magdalen College School choir (including her son Albert McIntosh aka Bertie), reached number 187 in the UK singles chart solely on album downloads, and was nominated for the International Press Academy's Satellite Award for 'Original Song in a Motion Picture' (2007). Apart from its intrinsic musical merits, the song can be interpreted as offering a corrective emotional fidelity to the source text that was sacrificed in the film's conclusion. One complaint at the adaptation was its removal of the novel's unsettling last three chapters (kept back for a putative sequel), and director Weitz acknowledged the 'marketing pressure' to provide a more family-friendly 'upbeat ending' (Charles McGrath, 'Unholy Production with a Fairy-Tale Ending', *New York Times*, 2 December 2007). This tonal lightening of the narrative denouement is counter-balanced by Bush's slow-paced and foreboding final soundscape (macro-modulating the film much as her closing chorus had micro-tempered *Lionheart*'s 'In Search of Peter Pan'), its ambient disturbance more acceptable to – or (if not staying for the credits) ignorable by – a young adult audience.

Alongside her film work, Bush was active in television, both through bespoke compositions and, much to fan excitement, appearing on-screen. Largely via her charity work for Comic Relief and Amnesty International, Bush had become friends with several leading contemporary comedy actors and accepted an invitation to contribute to the British television comedy showcase *The Comic Strip Presents* (C4/BBC 1982–1993). The series grew out of London's Comedy Store, centre of the new 'alternative comedy' movement that strove to avoid the racism, sexism, homophobia and religious intolerance then inherent in mainstream comedic acts both in clubs and on television. It was also a project similar to Bush's output in its plentiful cine-literacy as, over a decade, it realised for television 35 self-contained 'surreal, postmodern parodies' (Moy 2007: 62). Its main writer-performers comprised comedy double-acts Rik Mayall and Ade Edmondson, Dawn French and Jennifer Saunders, plus Nigel Planer and the project's guiding hand Peter Richardson (also co-director of 'The Sensual World' video, see Chapter 5). In addition, the series presented a plethora of regular and special star appearances ranging from Beryl Reid to Ruby Wax (Sangster and Condon 2005: 192).

Bush, an admirer of the series and collaborator with participants across several projects, made three bespoke contributions. The 33-minute cod-Hollywood blockbuster (series 4, episode 3) entitled *The*

Comic Strip Presents: GLC: The Carnage Continues... (BBC2, tx. 15 February 1990) again featured the 'Chinese box' format with *Comic Strip* actors playing Hollywood actors playing British politicians (e.g. Peter Richardson as Lee Van Cleef as Labour MP Tony Benn; Jennifer Saunders as Brigitte Nielsen as the Ice Maiden aka Conservative PM Margaret Thatcher). The episode was enhanced by Bush singing on the soundtrack her composition 'Ken', an up-beat number about London-based left-wing politician – and, according to her lyrics, 'funky sex machine' – Ken Livingstone (Robbie Coltrane playing Charles Bronson playing Ken).[3] The plot has Livingstone, elected leader of the Greater London Council (GLC), striving to prevent the evil Conservative party from flooding London so it can become a marina. Bush's 'Ken' parodies Isaac Hayes' Billboard chart-topping 'Theme From *Shaft*', the soul-funk signature song from 1971's breakout blaxploitation thriller directed by Gordon Parks, and its stirring call-and-response chorus ('Who is the leader of the GLC?' 'KEN!') accompanies a montage of Livingstone, who here has given up politics for a quiet riverside life, putting himself through a rigorous election campaign, alternating the compulsory kissing of babies with breaking allies out of prison and supplying them with sub-machine guns. His election allure is extra-diegetically augmented by Bush's stirring endorsement. Bush also wrote two instrumental tracks for the episode, 'One Last Look Around the House Before We Go' and 'The Confrontation'.[4]

Bush would again provide a number, 'Home for Christmas', for the 28-minute festive special *The Comic Strip Presents: Wild Turkey* (BBC2, tx. 24 December 1992). This (less successful) single-set episode loosely riffs on the Christmas Eve-set action film *Die Hard* (John McTiernan, 1988) where Bruce Willis' NYPD detective John McClane, seeking reconciliation with his estranged wife Holly (Bonnie Bedelia), must battle against Alan Rickman's German hostage-taking terrorist Hans Gruber. In the *Comic Strip* take, New York cop Jim (Paul Bartel) finds that the unplucked turkey he brings home to his wife Sue (Ruby Wax) is not just feathered but still alive: indeed, the bird aka 'Turk' (Phil Cornwell) takes the couple hostage in their high-rise apartment and, on learning the annual fate of his kind, demands the release of all caged turkeys. Sue's marriage to Jim is strained, and during the ensuing siege she bonds with Turk: as they watch *Peter Pan* on television Turk confesses to Sue, head resting on her shoulder, how he wishes he could fly. Admitting their feelings for each other, Sue and Turk briefly dance together to Bush's upbeat number, sung to a simple guitar accompaniment and brass solo. The song offers a cosy soundscape of Yuletide union and maintains Bush's accord with J.M. Barrie's idealism – jumping from the window Turk does not plummet to his death (like Gruber) but takes wing, heeding Sue's Wendy-like entreaty that 'you can fly if you really believe'. Bush's song is reprised in full over the closing credits, but now the notion that 'I would fly to you' if possessed of wings melancholically recalls Jim and Sue's avian-induced siege and final separation – Jim is appalled that Sue has 'gone beyond the law: the law of Man, and the law of Nature'. Ambivalence again mixes with idealism.[5]

In a unique career move, between these soundtrack offerings Bush took her *Comic Strip* adherence further by taking on an acting role. This came in *The Comic Strip Presents: Les Dogs* (BBC2, tx. 8 March 1990), a 28-minute television programme (series 4, episode 6) that plays like a cinematic mash-up of Sam Peckinpah with Federico Fellini – plus another dash of Stanley Kubrick. Bush made no musical contribution this time – that was provided by the titular Dogs, a Kiss-cloned French glam-metal band led by Kevin Allen. Instead she played the role of young bride Angela Watkins née Foster (with Alexei Sayle and Miranda Richardson as her parents, Daniel Peacock as groom Geoffrey, Tim McInnerny and Julie T. Wallace as his parents), whose hotel reception degenerates from inter-family insults to gun-fuelled bloodbath. Meanwhile, businessman Victor (Peter Richardson, also director and co-writer with Pete Richens) awakes from an episode-opening car crash that leaves his chauffeur dead and wanders into the reception: he is immediately asked to take the wedding photographs and drifts off into fantasises about rescuing, eloping with and visiting the beautiful bride until, with the couple about to kiss, Angela's eyes become dazzling headlights, and the sound of a car crash ends the film. Reviews were largely positive, though Tom Bussmann, singling out 'a splendidly disgusting Danny Peacock and much put-upon Kate Bush', seemed to criticise exam boards desperately seeking contemporary relevance as much as laud the episode's intricacies when he adjudged that 'The plot will no doubt be studied in the 1992 A-level syllabus' (*Guardian*, 9 March 1990). It wasn't, but nonetheless here follows a concise student study guide.

Les Dogs may seek its humour from blatant juxtapositions – amidst their reception-room shoot out, guests are mindful to maintain social proprieties (happy to move a badly parked car or offer directions to the toilet) – but all is conveyed in classic realist mode until Victor spies a young child cycling in the hotel corridor, a clear allusion to *The Shining*. Thereafter all becomes doggedly surreal as Angela re-appears in the honeymoon suite, now the child's mother in a black dress (plus red rubber gloves signifying domesticity), and informs Victor how she is all set for them to run away together. Seemingly years have passed as 'uncle' Victor joins Angela plus family for Christmas dinner, and finally, sporting a Santa Claus outfit, he steals into the Watkins bedroom to bestow a kiss on Angela as she sleeps next to the still besotted Geoffrey. These closing seconds, as Angela awakens and transforms into the exposition's accident, reveal the preceding half-hour as literally surreal – the compressed imaginings of a dying man. *Les Dogs*, it emerges (not far removed from Bush's 'The Ninth Wave'), has enacted with its foreshadowing implausibilities a *Comic Strip* variant on the increasingly off-key experiences of apparent car-crash survivor Mary Henry (Candace Hilligoss) in the American horror film *Carnival of Souls* (Herk Harvey, 1962). This is a celebrated example, like the final act of Gilliam's *Brazil*, of the structural trope termed 'false narrative continuation' or 'deathbed fantasy' (Strank 2014: 177), a twist-in-the-tale ending that forces viewers to question all they have previously seen. The films of Harvey and Gilliam (and Adrian Lyne's concurrent *Jacob's Ladder* (1990)) all have an acknowledged narrative debt to the Cannes and Academy Award-winning French short *La Rivière du Hibou* / (literally) *Owl River* (Robert Enrico, 1962) and its dark surprise ending (Goodall et al. 2009: 18). Enrico's film in turn is based on (and in English named after) the ur-text of dying fantasy narratives, Ambrose Bierce's Civil War short story 'An Occurrence at Owl Creek Bridge' (1890), where condemned Confederate soldier Peyton Farquar believes he has escaped the Union soldiers' rope around his neck (mistakenly, the final sentence tells us).[6] Intertextually naming the episode *Les Dogs* offers a potential nod to the influential French short version with its animal title (Enrico's film is also 28 minutes long). Intratextually the name adds a potent structural coherence as we belatedly recall how, at the outset, Victor's Jaguar had crashed into the metal band's grey transport van, and realise that 'Les Dogs', spray-painted in large red letters along its side, constitutes not just an integrated credit title but an integral plot point, a cue to this visualised dilation of the moment of death.

And Bush? Though the opening credits are listed alphabetically (placing Bush second), she is undoubtedly the stand-out name in the cast. A literal fantasy figure throughout the episode, her attire and status as object of desire render Bush principally a refulgent star presence for the diegetic (and extra-diegetic) male gaze (Figure 3.2). But she also acts well. Partly a corollary of the absence of female agency in a traditional Christian wedding service, the relative passivity of Angela's character is here, while not ideologically defensible, artistically advantageous. Film and television have, by and large, been dominated

Figure 3.2 Les Dogs – The Bride Wore White.

by a 'verisimilar' style of acting: modelled on everyday behaviour, this restrained, understated performance mode, sometimes termed 'invisible acting', allows amplification of individualised gestures to come from the close, quasi-forensic attention of the film camera. Here, unlike with her overblown performance as the white-gowned bride in her television presentation of 'The Wedding List', Bush is, with Richardson's guidance, more muted in bodily and facial movements, almost a mesmerising still centre as, amidst the gun-fire mayhem, she calmly accepts Geoffrey's chocolate-smeared embraces, cheerily tries out novelty wedding presents, and convincingly mimes unconsciousness as Victor carries her into the honeymoon suite. When the bride wears black and assumes a more active role, Bush delivers her lines about leaving her husband for Victor – 'I haven't told him about Dorset: did you mention anything?' – with a credible quiet and breathy collusion. Though she never showed the inclination (or confidence) thereafter to pursue a straight acting career, Bush's performance here, alongside Richardson a foil to the more theatrically projecting *Comic Strip* collective, reveals a charismatic screen presence of preternatural beauty with a mimetic potential never developed. *Les Dogs* shows the road (alas) not taken.

Les Dogs saw Bush separating her screen acting from musical contributions: by now, though, she had combined these twin roles (and added direction to her credits) in her music video productions. This important medium in her work is examined in Part 2.

Notes

1 An edited version of 'Be Kind to My Mistakes' appeared on 1997's re-release of *Hounds of Love*.
2 The song's use in the television drama *Walk Away and I Stumble* (ITV, tx. 14 November 2005) led to it reaching number 3 in the UK Official Download Chart. It has subsequently featured in *A Man Called Otto* (Marc Forster, 2022) and *The Mother* (Niki Caro, 2023), again prompting entry to the UK's Download top 40. Since 2005 the song has regularly featured in adverts for the UK's National Society for the Prevention of Cruelty to Children charity. The 1997 cover by R&B singer Maxwell, itself a Billboard 200 entry, featured in *Love & Basketball* (Gina Prince-Bythewood, 2000).
3 Coltrane had already worked with Bush, providing one of the disembodied voices trying to rouse the protagonist on 'Waking the Witch'. On their 2011 collaboration for 'Deeper Understanding', see Chapter 4.
4 'Ken' would become the B-side to 1990's 'Love and Anger' single. (The two instrumental tracks were also included on the 12" and CD single).
5 'Home for Christmas' would become the B-side to two single releases from *The Red Shoes*: Bush's UK 12" 'Moments of Pleasure' and America's 'Rubberband Girl'.
6 The film of *An Occurrence at Owl Creek Bridge* gained further traction when aired as series 5, episode 22 (CBS, tx. 28 February 1964) of *The Twilight Zone* anthology series (1959–1964).

Part 2
Video

4 Moments of Pleasure
Kate Bush as Music Video Performer

Bush's performance in *Les Dogs* is notable for its appropriateness to the medium. It must be admitted, however, that elsewhere her acting style was not always scaled down to fit the 'realism' or 'verisimilitude' habitual on film and television representation. This is especially true in several of her early music videos, the medium into which she funnelled her imagination as she eschewed the stress and fatigue inherent in elaborate live performances. David Sinclair noted that, straight from 'Wuthering Heights', opinion was polarised:

> To many she was an artist of pure, idiosyncratic talent, a fragile beauty, possibly a genius. To others her ululating singing style, and the eccentric displays of amateur dramatics which seemed so integral to her performance, were as comforting as the feel of silver paper on a newly filled tooth.
>
> ('A–Z Guide to Rock', *Times*, 9 December 1989)[1]

Rather than this mutually opposed stance I would argue that, in postmodern style, both readings are possible across her early video performances.

A strong strand in Bush's promo video work has been the recording of dance. The initial key contributor here was Keith MacMillan aka Keef (1934–2012), photographer, sleeve-designer and pioneering music video director. Alongside the already-examined 'Wuthering Heights' and 'Hammer Horror' (see Chapter 2), MacMillan was the go-to director for Bush's studio-set videos through to 1980, works that, with Bush still 'finding her feet', reveal strikingly different levels of achievement in the medium. For 'The Man with the Child in His Eyes', (her second single release, on 26 May 1978, hitting number 6 in the UK and 85 in her first US Billboard entry), Bush is more openly sexualised than with 'Wuthering Heights', in a gold-spangled skin-tight outfit, but

DOI: 10.4324/9781003479604-6

throughout an imaginatively choreographed piece she remains seated and, with occasional image doubling, uses only her upper body to cut slow and sinuous shapes that fill the screen.[2] By contrast, 'Them Heavy People' (a May 1978 A-side release in Japan) employs a wildly overplayed routine that is not only more suited to the (am dram) stage than video format, but also betrays the song's paeon to spiritual teachers with a lame pastiche of shoulder-shaking gangsters in trench coats and trilbies, the result more Harry Worth than Humphrey Bogart.

Another lip-synched performance video, 1979's 'Wow', at least stayed true to the song's showbiz context with Bush being 'alone on the stage tonight', but in the spotlight-backed chorus it reuses what was already becoming a formulaic image doubling, while Bush again over-emphasises in delivery and facial expressions. At best a proficient effort, it also fell foul of the BBC censors for Bush tapping her rear while singing about a male actor and his Vaseline lubricant, and was later dropped from her videography.[3] Against this, 'Babooshka' (her second UK top 5 hit, released on 27 June 1980) can be assessed as an accomplished transitional piece, visually creative in its choreography for the song's narrative of a woman who tests her husband's fidelity by adopting a younger alter-ego identity. A common theme in English folk songs – Bush cites the influence of the Cecil Sharp-collected 'Sovay' aka 'The Female Highwayman' (Irwin 1980: 29) – her variant shows her artistic unpredictability by eschewing an (expected) feminist take and condemning the wife's jealous actions for irreparably damaging the marriage. In the video, scenes where Bush, demurely veiled and wearing a black bodysuit, dances with a double-bass prop (representing her passive husband) alternate, during the chorus, with Bush, again highly sexualised, backlit as a chainmail-bikinied sword-wielding warrior queen (and embodiment of the castration complex). While anticipating sword and sci-fi/sorcery fare like *She-Ra: Princess of Power* (Filmation/Mattel, 1985–1987) and *Red Sonja* (Richard Fleischer, 1985), Bush's battle costume (acknowledged on *The Single File* video collection) was based not on moving images but on Chris Achilléos' Corgi paperback cover illustration for Richard Kirk's 1978 adult fantasy novel *Raven – Swordsmistress of Chaos*.[4]

These and later dance pieces from Bush – plus the Bowie-esque *gesamtkunstwerk* of her stage appearances (MacMillan also directed *Kate Bush Live at the Hammersmith Odeon*, an hour-long highlights package of her 13 May 1979 'Tour of Life' concert, released on home video in 1981) – can display high skill in their use of movement and mise-en-scène, but they are briefly treated here since, not discernibly film or television-influenced, they lie beyond the focus of this study. Nonetheless, it needs emphasising that MacMillan's music videos, despite their varied settings and personae (and artistic success), helped to define a consistent visual identity for Bush, one that may have polarised public opinion but which is cogently – because oxymoronically – defined by Jason Anderson as a 'genteel eroticism' (2022: 116).[5]

However, the promo videos for singles bracketing 'Babooskha' confirm a shift in both ambition and sophistication. Progressing from the straightforward arm-swinging of 'Wow' and the hoodlum schtick of 'Them Heavy People' to more narrative-driven pieces, this development is evident in MacMillan's direction of the doleful military manoeuvres of 'Army Dreamers', and especially the psychodrama of 'Breathing' (both 1980). These two numbers move towards a broad political, anti-war message, admittedly conveyed through character emotion rather than offering any structural critique of society, while, indicative of a concomitant move towards the filmic, their accompanying videos were both made on location, at Black Park, Windsor, a regular haunt for Hammer horror shoots including Terence Fisher's *The Curse of Frankenstein* (1957) and *Dracula: Prince of Darkness* (1966).

'Army Dreamers' (a number 16 UK hit when released on 22 September 1980 as *Never for Ever*'s third and final single) is a slow waltz with folk-song texture that tells of an Irish-accented mother wrestling with guilt and grieving for her enlisted teenage son, accidentally killed while serving overseas. The video offers a quasi-literal if stylised representation of the song's narrative, with Bush portraying a mourning but military-active mother – a conflation of roles that muddies the song's anti-militaristic tendencies.[6] It begins with a close-up on Bush, dressed in combat uniform but holding a blond male child who wanders off-screen, returning moments later in army camouflage (Figure 4.1). Bush and a small company of (bandmate) soldiers next make their way through woodland, several falling backwards when hit by explosives. Bush as mother again reaches out for her soldier son, but he disappears. Finally, running towards the camera, Bush herself is blown up.

The visualisation has its positives, despite the role confusion. The mother sighting her soldier child behind a tree, dropping her rifle and running forward only to find he has disappeared, is played out three times, the last with the son now an adult: the repetition intimates the psychological trauma of an unresolvable and time-expanding remembrance of lost ones. There is an effective intertextuality when we notice a soldier's rifle butt stencilled with 'KTB', the monogram Bush employed in her early gigs with the KT Bush Band: it offers a poignant contrast to the song's chorus on how the army hoovers up the UK's uneducated proletariat (when the chorus suggests he could have been a rock star instead, the mother plaintively replies that he could not afford a guitar).

52 *Video*

Figure 4.1 'Army Dreamers' – The Boy in the Bush.

The video's explicitly cinematic effects have more mixed results: there are dramatically achieved hand-held shots of running soldiers, but its (over-used) slow-motion depictions of their explosive deaths weakly pastiche Sam Peckinpah's *Cross of Iron* (1977). In a transitional video for Bush, the musical impulse and mimetic setting can fail to cohere, its undermining by an over-determined choreography exemplified by the opening close-up of Bush blinking in three-quarter time to the Fairlight-sampled sounds of rifles being bolted. Overall, Ron Moy finds that 'the subtlety of the song is swamped by the visuals' and that Bush 'cannot resist the elaborate pouts, unrealistic miming and wide-eyed stares at camera that on occasions render her performances over-dramatic and "hammy"' (2007: 96). Steve Binnie, recalling *Monty Python*, (harshly) finds the whole 'choreographed combat manoeuvres in strict waltz tempo ... hard to watch without expecting Graham Chapman's Colonel to appear in shot, crying "Stop that! It's silly!"' (2016: 182).

'Breathing' could, if so minded, be seen as equally silly, but for this viewer it offers a more assured if abstracted shift from dance to narrative. In the song, Bush assumes the persona of a fully sentient (and, since reincarnated, knowledgeable) foetus already absorbing nicotine from its smoking mother but more fearful of (re-)entering a world now experiencing nuclear fallout – in the background a scarily matter-of-fact (male-voiced) official broadcast instructs people how to differentiate between 'a small nuclear explosion and a large one' by counting its flash duration. The closing track on *Never for Ever* and a brave/controversial choice as its lead single (a 4.53 edit released 14 April 1980), the song's melodic sweep and vocal crescendo helped it reach number 16 in the UK.

Armageddon was in the airwaves: Bush had just shared the chorus on Peter Gabriel's February 1980 release 'Games Without Frontiers', a top 4 UK hit which, treating superpower brinkmanship, carried the same charge of nuclear anxiety. Rather than Gabriel, however, Bush stated that her song was tonally inspired by Pink Floyd's *The Wall* (evident in the outro), and its information derived from watching a television documentary about the effects of nuclear war (Irwin 1980: 29). Though unnamed, this was undoubtedly the recent *Panorama* programme, 'If the Bomb Drops' (BBC1, tx. 11 March 1980), which, narrated by Jeremy Paxman, explored the British government's preparations (or lack thereof) for a nuclear attack, and demonstrated the effects of thermonuclear explosions on the human body by flash-roasting pig carcasses. As Rob Young notes, 'Rapid cuts between footage of shocked and surprised humans and the seared, melted meat are, to say the least, disconcerting' (2021: 84). From such unprepossessing material Bush composed a number that marked a distinct progression in her artistic ambitions, creating an affective politics and harbinger of the experimental works on *The Dreaming* and beyond. In interview Bush told Kris Needs that 'From my own viewpoint that's the best thing I've ever written. It's the best thing I've ever produced', and emphasised how the visual element was important to its realisation: 'It's almost like the mother's stomach is a big window that's like a cinema screen, and they're seeing all this terrible chaos' ('Fire in the Bush', *ZigZag*, August 1980).

This ready correlation between sound and vision, and the song's combination of life creation and destruction, is realised in the two-part ('in' and 'out') video that eschews previously derided pouts and wide-eyed stares by keeping the singer's face mostly out of focus then staying with mid- or long-shots. In the video's first act, Bush, covered in clear plastic, portrays the embryo, complete with umbilical cord and confined to a large plastic bubble/amniotic sac, pushing rhythmically at the wall of what is both a source of refuge and vulnerability (Figure 4.2). After the fatalistic second verse (bemoaning how 'We've lost our chance'), the song's bridge sees the image blur as Bush tumbles from this transparent womb: the transition to the outside world is policed by two white-clad figures with sun faces (cut-out masks like that worn by Delius, though

Figure 4.2 'Breathing' – The Girl in the Bubble.

here (unintentionally) bathetic in effect).[7] There follows no celebration of birth or infant purity as immediately a blast of atomic light (as described in the government announcement) flashes on Bush and seven (band) adults, all in hazmat suits who, as the final chorus wonders what sacrifices lie ahead, stagger on a hillside then wade through (presumably contaminated) water, the environment now so bombarded with radiation their faces have turned green. As the song ends, the camera moves in on Bush, alone white-faced and with arms outstretched to keep her balance (an image influential on David Bowie's *Ashes to Ashes* video, shot in May 1980?). A silent 25-second coda (cut from BBC airings) presents the reverse-shot of a mushroom cloud that leads into Bush and her band lounging on the grass.

Rather than a return to a *Lionheart* arcadia, however, the eight characters singularly fail to respond to a further explosive flash, indicative of their resignation to this now irreversible radioactive environment with its giant deformed mushrooms and tainted human faces. Citing Joseph Masco's identification of how the atomic bomb has created a new cognitive orientation towards everyday life (2005), Jean-Thomas Tremblay cogently interprets this desensitised epilogue as enacting 'the "nuclear uncanny": the shift in "perceptual space" or sum of "material effects, psychic tension, and sensory confusion" brought about by nuclear warfare' (2022: 63). Bush's final turn to stare into the camera contrasts with her opening intrauterine energy and admonishes in its seeming listlessness. The screen slowly whites out, concluding an accomplished and activist work.[8]

Bush, exponentially ambitious but always self-critical, differentiated less than others in her delight at both videos. Of 'Army Dreamers' she proudly declared to Doug Pringle that it 'work[ed] beautifully' and 'For me that's the closest I've got to a little bit of film' (*Profiles in Rock*, CITY-TV Canada, December 1980), while she later averred to Steve Sutherland that 'Ever since "Breathing" I've wanted to make videos like little films' ('Video Heights', *Melody Maker*, 3 December 1983). Wherever the turning point, one can sense Bush, now musically autonomous, straining also to increase control of the filming process. These two pieces signalled the end, after nine videos, of the Bush–MacMillan partnership and a shift in emphasis that would culminate in self-realised and narrative-led visual productions.

The visual accompaniment to most of Bush's subsequent musical productions takes on those desired characteristics of 'little films'. Initially, though, her post-MacMillan releases reverted largely to the dance template. The promo videos for *The Dreaming*'s singles, 'Sat in Your Lap' (issued 21 June 1981 and a number 11 UK hit) with its roller-skating dunces, harlequins and minotaurs, plus 'Suspended in Gaffa', set in an old barn with an appearance from Bush's mother, Hannah, were entrusted to Brian Wiseman, editor of the *Hammersmith Odeon* concert video. Between these, artwork designer Paul Henry directed 'The Dreaming' where space-suited Bush strides across a studio mock-up Australia, and the (already discussed) cod-heist of 'There Goes a Tenner'. These promo videos can be adjudged a directorial apprenticeship for Bush, increasingly controlling their creation but still learning the necessities of visual media – Henry, for example, knowing the need to instil on-screen momentum, recalls having to dissuade Bush from filming 'The Dreaming' entirely in wide-shot to show off its dance routine (Doyle 2022: 151). Also, while eclectic in subject matter and design, these pieces reveal another shift in Bush's moving images, stepping away from Lindsay Kemp's mime influence (though he would return in *TLTC&TC*) and employing instead the interpretive dance choreography of her new mentor-teacher Dyane Gray-Cullert, a disciple of modern dance pioneer Martha Graham.

This developed dance style, the subjective translating of the human condition and its emotions into rhythmic, fluid bodily movement, is best exemplified in what Bush intended to be her farewell to dance promos, the 4.55-minute video for the *Hounds of Love* lead single

'Running Up That Hill'. Martha Graham repeatedly termed the practising dancer 'an athlete of God' (1991: 3) and, for the song initially called 'A Deal with God' (until the probability of Christian countries' censorship intervened), Bush sought to counter a perceived trend for demeaning dance as a mere accessory in pop videos. In interview with J.J. Jackson, she expressed her aim to create 'an almost classical piece of dance, filmed as well as possible, because it's rarely filmed well now' ('X-Ray', *MTV*, November 1985). To this end, she worked on choreography with Gray-Cullert and dancer Michael (later Misha) Hervieu (regular partner Stuart Arnold was not available).[9] For the filming, Bush, undeterred by her disappointments with *Brazil*, sought assistance from Terry Gilliam: he passed on directing but recommended his regular cameraman (also cameraman on *Pink Floyd: The Wall* (Alan Parker, 1982)), David Garfath.

Jason Anderson terms the resultant video 'a triumph by any measure – indeed there may be no other music video that so powerfully demonstrate[s] dance's ability to convey both story and emotion' (2022: 116). It is certainly artistically accomplished. To complement the twirling arms and body-entwining dance moves, plus the innovative costume design rendering Bush and Hervieu almost interchangeable in identical grey hakamas, Garfath adopted a fittingly fluid camerawork and muted colour pallet. Also, while arrestingly dance-oriented, the video's final section, enacting the difficulty of shedding a given gender identity, gestures to a cinematic narrative and mise-en-scène of social conformity and fear. It recalls the crowded urban dystopia of *Metropolis* (Fritz Lang, 1927) as the couple are separated in corridors filled with marching figures, all wearing cut-out photograph masks of the faces of Bush or Hervieu. Bush's desperate reaching out also parallels the conclusion to Hitchcock's Cold War thriller *Torn Curtain* (1966), where British scientist Sarah Sherman (Julie Andrews) is pulled away from her fiancé Michael Armstrong (Paul Newman) by a panic-stricken theatre audience (Figure 4.3). But a triumph by any measure? Not commercially: the bespoke music video channel MTV baulked at its non-conformist nature and substituted a safer choreographed performance given on BBC1's talk show *Wogan* (tx. 5 August 1985).

After this swan song to dance, Bush became fully cinematic in her next promo video, 'Cloudbusting' (1985): with a full narrative arc and star casting, Rob Young asserts it 'plays like a silent film' (2011: 571). Here Bush worked directly with Gilliam to conceive and loosely storyboard the visual correlation for a cello-driven number with esoteric lyrics that, released as *Hounds of Love*'s

Figure 4.3 'Running Up That Hill' – Lost in the Bush.

second single on 14 October 1985, reached number 20 in the UK charts. Inspired by Peter Reich's 1973 memoir *A Book of Dreams*, Bush's composition concerns young Peter's loving relationship with his father Wilhelm Reich (1897–1957), the controversial Austrian psychoanalyst and Freud disciple who fled his Nazi-occupied homeland for America in 1939 to continue his research into body therapy and life energy aka 'orgonomy', and who, later beloved of 1968 student protesters, is accredited with creating the term 'the sexual revolution' (Strick 2015: 2). In Bush's song, conflating incidents from summer 1953 and August 1956, Peter recalls life on the family home/ranch/research centre named Orgonon, where father and son worked together on creating the Cloudbuster, a ray-gun-like machine to suck down atmospheric orgone into cloud formations for 'making rain'. However, his father's research constitutes 'a threat to the men in power' (America's Food and Drug Administration (FDA)) who abruptly arrive at the property and arrest Wilhelm.

Gilliam, again declining to direct, now proposed Julian Doyle, his collaborator on special effects photography and editing for the *Monty Python* films, *Time Bandits* (Gilliam, 1981) and *Brazil*. The resultant video, a contender for Bush's best-known contribution to the genre, featured the singer, sporting a short wig and ragamuffin attire, as pre-teen Peter, while Reich, in a casting coup, was played by future (2017) Honorary Academy Award winner Donald Sutherland. Particularly impressed by his role as grieving parent John Baxter in Nicolas Roeg's psychodrama *Don't Look Now* (1973) – alongside *Time Bandits* one of 'Kate's Desert Island Films' (see Appendix), Bush directly approached Sutherland who was in England filming the (commercially disastrous) historical drama *Revolution* (Hugh Hudson, 1985): the Canadian-born actor agreed to work without pay during a three-day break (thus obviating work visa obstacles). Filmed under clear blue skies at Oxfordshire's Vale of White Horse for a cost of just over £100,000 (mostly spent on adding clouds post-production), the promo features a longer (6.57-minute) 'video mix' version of 'Cloudbusting' (eventually released on April 1994's CD single of 'The Red Shoes'), and significantly shifts the song's perspective – and hence acting weight – to Wilhelm/Sutherland. It begins by showing father and son climbing to the top of Dragon Hill (the famed Uffington White Horse is briefly visible) and testing out the Cloudbuster machine. When Wilhelm leaves Peter on the machine and returns home, he recalls in flashback their working happily together on various projects, until government officials storm his lab. Peter, sensing danger, arrives too late and can only watch helplessly as his father is bundled into the back of a 'big black car' and driven away. Peter runs back to the Cloudbuster and successfully activates it, much to the delight of Wilhelm who, watching from the rear window, sees it begin to rain.

The video also delighted Peter Reich (Bush sent him a completed VHS copy): in interview he told Alex Denney that 'Quite magically, this British musician had tapped precisely into a unique and magical fulfilment of father-son devotion, emotion and understanding. They had captured it all' ('The Story Behind Kate Bush's *Cloudbusting* Video', *Dazed*, 30 October 2016).[10] Critics too have commended the work as exemplary, at both theoretical and emotional levels. Kevin Donnelly highlights its micro-narrative and intermeshing of sound and allusive imagery as indicative of 'the central importance for music in postmodern culture' (1994: 44); for Jason Anderson 'The result stands as one of the most dramatically compelling, visually exquisite and ultimately heartbreaking videos in the history of the medium' (2022: 116).

How so this combination? Cinematically, the overarching influence of *Brazil* is evident in the video's binary of rural escape versus dark-suited officialdom. More specifically, the early premonition of approaching agents and Wilhelm's arrest rearranges chronological and causal editing in a manner resonant of Nicolas Roeg, as in the opening to *Performance* (1970). The shot of agents' feet marching down the FDA building's stone steps explicitly references the soldiers' descent of the Odessa Steps in *Battleship Potemkin* (Sergei Eisenstein, 1925). The Cloudbuster itself, in reality relatively streamlined, is here a huge steampunk machine: while reminiscent of Gilliam's animation style, it was devised by members of the team that worked on the xenomorph in *Alien*, and its outer curves and inner extension can be read as similarly combining female and male sexual imagery. Nonetheless, beneath the allusions one can conjecture a cloaked autobiography. Bush's own father, Robert, a GP and amateur pianist, fostered his daughter's imagination, much as we see Wilhelm encouraging young Peter's drawings – and Sutherland's physical appearance is far closer to Dr Bush than Dr Reich. Personal experience again resides within postmodern technique.

Intratextually, the video works (less successfully) to pick up on the song's setting and source. Though the Reichs' home was in Maine, we see newspaper cuttings from the orthographically approximate *Oregon Times*; as the pair hug on the hilltop, young Peter/Bush archly pulls out an anachronistic copy of *A Book of Dreams* from the father's overcoat. Arguably, however, the biggest obstacle, if not to verisimilitude then the suspension of disbelief, remains the gender-flipped performance of Bush herself. First there is the sound: typical of this more intimate, mature album, Bush's voice is here a rich alto – rather than conveying adolescence, Ann Powers rightly terms it 'almost maternal' (2022). Then there is the vision: while the acting style is again toned down and thus more emotionally convincing – although she overdoes the child's doting grinning, her distraught reactions as Wilhelm is driven away strike as more method than mannered – no amount of short spiked hair, stripy knitwear, dungarees, or even placing 6 ft 4 in Sutherland on a box, could make Bush look convincingly like a short pre-pubescent male (Figure 4.4). Gamine perhaps, but swapping places here only exacerbates problems of credibility (and Peter's shirt buttons right over left). Even for the otherwise supportive Anderson it constitutes a 'not-inconsiderable flaw': he further notes Bush's own (typical) self-deprecation: '"I looked a bit like Coco the clown," she'd later admit' (2022: 116).[11]

Graeme Thomson terms 'Cloudbusting' as 'in many ways ... a small, self-contained film in its own right' (2015: 272) – and so it proved. Alongside Bush's artistic admiration for the A-list actor, there had been hardnosed hopes that Sutherland would prove an entrée to

Figure 4.4 'Cloudbusting' – The Bush in the Boy.

American markets, but again MTV showed little interest in airing such an atypical example, its bucolic mise-en-scène and narrative development far removed from the already established 'MTV aesthetic' with a privileging of ostentatious camerawork and rapid-fire editing tempi that was already infiltrating longer film formats (Calavito 2007: 15–31). It also fell foul of BBC television's *Top of The Pops* and its definition of 'an acceptable video' for broadcast since it 'lacked synchronised vocal performance' (Caston 2020: 106). Stymied of small-screen airtime, agreement was reached instead for 'Cloudbusting' to be exhibited in UK cinemas as the support feature for another study of eccentric scientific invention, Amblin Entertainment's *Back to the Future* (Robert Zemeckis, 1985). Shown in 35 mm film projection and with full surround sound, the nostalgic affection in which the video for this minor hit is still held by many undoubtedly relates to its bracketing with the autumn's big-screen bestseller.[12]

Creative differences between Bush and Doyle at the editing stage (including discussions which decided against an afterword explaining how Reich was sentenced to two years imprisonment for contempt of court and died in jail) had led to Gilliam stepping in as mediator.[13]

Indicative of her growing confidence in the medium and improved technical know-how, 'Cloudbusting' prompted Bush to progress to solo-directing her videos, taking full control as she long had with musical production. The results are examined next.

Notes

1 The view has persisted: Suede's Brett Anderson, an admirer of Bush's work, considers her early performances those of an artist 'finding her way' and 'all a little bit am dram' (*The Kate Bush Story: Running Up That Hill*, BBC4, tx. 22 August 2014).
2 Jovanovich argues for the influence of Bush's choreography and costume on Britney Spears' 2003 'Toxic' video, directed by Joseph Kahn (2005: 78). Referencing her similar performance atop a piano on 1978's *Saturday Night Live*, Christopher Knowles proposes that Michelle Pfeiffer 'later stole the routine' in *The Fabulous Baker Boys* (Steve Kloves, 1989) (2010: 123).
3 For 1986's video compilation album *The Whole Story* a new version of 'Wow' (without the gesture to anal sex) was created from selected live performances.
4 Bush informed Peter Powell in interview that one source for the song title was seeing British comedy musical duo Flanders and Swann: 'I turned on the television and there was Donald Swann singing about Babooshka' (*Never for Ever Debut*, BBC Radio 1, 11 October 1980).
5 These early videos' ripeness for parody was exemplified by comedian Pamela Stephenson, who emphasised eroticism before gentility in Peter Brewis' spoof of 'Them Heavy People', entitled 'Oh England My Leotard'. Stephenson fights off groping hands while singing how 'People bought my latest hits / Cos they liked my latex tits / Everyone is trying hard / To get inside my leotard' (*Not The Nine O'Clock News*, series 3, episode 2, BBC2, tx. 11 March 1980).
6 A clearer demarcation of roles (if arguably patronising in class depiction) was established in the performance of 'Army Dreamers' on German television's *RockPop* (ZDF, tx. 13 September 1980), where Bush, dressed as Mrs Mop, a stereotyped cleaning lady complete with head-scarf and rubber gloves, swept the stage and danced around combat-dressed band members.
7 More effective in its solar imagery, the video to Bush's 1986 duet with Peter Gabriel, 'Don't Give Up', (a UK number 9 hit), directed by Kevin Godley and Lol Creme, consists of a single take of the singers embracing while, behind them, a large sun enters total eclipse then re-emerges. Bush later recorded another duet, with Larry Adler on George and Ira Gershwin's 'The Man I Love'. Reaching number 27 in the UK following its 18 July 1994 release as lead single for *The Glory of Gershwin* album, it was accompanied by a stylised and traditional black-and-white performance video, again directed by Godley.
8 Bush donated the song to *Greenpeace – The Album*, released in June 1985 as a fundraising vehicle for the environmental organisation.
9 Life imitating art? In 1993 Hervieu took the name Misha and eventually underwent gender reassignment surgery.
10 'Cloudbusting' also pleased English EDM duo Utah Saints, who sampled Bush's chorus for their May 1992 single 'Something Good', a UK number 4 hit. The accompanying video featured scenes from Doyle's 'Cloudbusting'.

11 Reich's research – and the US government's crackdown – also inform Serbian avant-garde filmmaker Dusan Makavejev's renowned (and banned) *W.R.: Mysteries of the Organism / W.R. - Misterije Organizma* (1971).
12 The song's enduring association with the psychoanalyst is evidenced in its use on the Austrian documentary *Who's Afraid of Wilhelm Reich? / Wer hat Angst vor Wilhelm Reich?* (Antonin Svoboda, 2009).
13 When permissions were sought to include 'Running Up That Hill' and 'Cloudbusting' on the video compilation *Power to the People: British Music Videos 1966–2016*, it was agreed to credit Bush as co-director 'to reflect the true extent of her work on the videos' (Caston 2020: 84). Other sources (as of March 2024) still record Garfath and Doyle as sole directors.

5 This Woman's Work
Kate Bush as Music Video Director

Acknowledging the dangers in attributing auteur status to directors in such a collaborative medium, Graeme Thomson nonetheless contends that 'a clear unity of style' emerges from Bush's efforts behind the camera: 'the videos are heavily stylised, dramatic and rather stagey' (2015: 275). This study argues that 'stagey' can increasingly be replaced by 'cinematic' and/or 'televisual', since any abiding unity will be shown to come from the shaping intertextuality and direct references that abound in her visual works, illustrative of the music-centred 'relationship of mutual influence' between film/television and pop videos in postmodern culture (Donnelly 1994: 44).[1]

This trait is evident from Bush's first solo direction, the promo video to accompany the 24 February 1986 release of 'Hounds of Love', which reached number 18 in the UK charts. A contributing factor to this minor success may have been the 3-minute video which again only received limited air-play by eschewing lip-synch mode – another common trait of Bush as director was never to kowtow to mainstream commercial expectation. The video opens in a wide museum space where an initially bespectacled Girl (Bush) makes eye contact with The Man (Gow Hunter) as fedora-clad agents attempt to arrest him: breaking free, he reaches the Girl and pulls her after him. They run through moonlit woodland, now handcuffed together, until they enter a brightly lit party and dance until, surrounded by agents, they again escape.

The song is generally interpreted as being about the fear of falling in love and entering a serious relationship, a feeling that can resemble being chased by a pack of hounds, but one that might well be worth overcoming: 'perhaps these baying hounds are really friendly', Bush has glossed (*Kate Bush Club Newsletter*, 18, 1985). Here she finds a cinematic correlation for the musical metaphor. Though sampling *Night of the Demon* and informed by *Gone to Earth* (see Chapter 2), her directing debut focuses instead on a stylish homage to Alfred

DOI: 10.4324/9781003479604-7

Hitchcock, notably his loose adaptation of John Buchan's 1915 novel *The 39 Steps* (1935), where falsely accused Richard Hannay (Robert Donat) becomes embroiled in preventing a spy-ring from stealing British military secrets. In interview Bush termed Hitchcock 'a genius', 'completely revolutionary' and, while emphasising that she could never emulate him, 'a tremendous influence on me whenever I'm making a video – he's really the ultimate reference point' (*The Sensual World of Kate Bush*, VH-1, January 1990). Not all have seen the influence as beneficial: Ian Cawood questions, with 'Hounds of Love', 'Why a song, already laden with strong visual metaphors and the inspiration of two celebrated films, needed a completely different intertextual reference', and offers an unequivocal answer: 'Bush's directorial naivety as well as her well-attested impetuousness' (2016: 56).

This is harsh. There are moments of cliché (the liberated Girl literally letting her hair down), and the chase, while visually dynamic, can fail to match the driving beat of the music. However, shaped by set-piece allusions rather than following a consistent narrative causality (handcuffs come and go, for instance, weakening their force as a metaphor for union/marriage), Bush's elliptical video picks up resonantly on several key tropes from Hitchcock's film and offers an effective new framing for the central theme. It begins with the (innocent) man forced to run, a persistent narrative in Hitchcock films, e.g. *North by Northwest* (1959). The Man evading his captors, pulling the Girl after him – matched to the line 'Here I go' – and their woodland flight, all parallel Hannay's handcuffed escape across the Scottish Highlands with the initially reluctant Pamela (Madeleine Carroll). The video's slow dancing section echoes how, on reaching Scotland, Hannay visits the house of spy-leader Professor Jordan (Godfrey Tearle) who is hosting a (more restrained) party. Betrayed, indeed left for dead, Hannay effects a further escape, as does the Man, here joined by Bush/the Girl. Additionally, and an effective touch, as the pair first flee, amongst those rushing to the door to watch is a Hitchcock lookalike, a homage to the director's penchant for making cameo appearances in his films.

There are, though, significant shifts in tone and focus. *Night of the Demon* is not forgotten as the dark lighting and deep shadows framing the duo's escape recall Tourneur's film, notably the pursuit of American psychologist John Holden (Dana Andrews) by the manifesting demon. The video thus stays with horror more than Hitchcock's film which, as Mark Glancy notes, gilds its spy narrative with in-vogue sparring-couple screwball comedy (2003: 27). In a regular Bush feature, her video also shifts the perspective: *The 39 Steps* is typical of Hitchcock in its 'optical subjectivity', a systematic filming style where, for

David Bordwell et al., 'the narration confines us to a single character's point of view to a greater degree than is normal' (1985: 79). Whereas Hitchcock privileges Hannay's viewpoint, Bush offers a greater objectivity, a fuller sharing of screen space and orientation – as arguably it must, with Bush the 'star' in this telling.

In so doing, the video determinedly offers greater female agency. Carroll's Pamela is considered a template for the career-long 'Hitchcock blonde', defined by the director himself as 'the type of woman, particularly the type of Englishwoman, who combined what François Truffaut described as a "cool surface" and "an inner fire"' awoken by the man's attention (White 2014: 186). Here Bush changes not just the woman's blondeness (she resembles far more the dark-haired beauty of *Gone to Earth*'s Jennifer Jones), but also her influence on the relationship. She initially portrays the stereotypical repressed 'librarian' (Figure 5.1), bespectacled with hair tied up ('I've always been a coward, and I don't know what's good for me,' she sings), but her partnership is more consensual than initially in Hitchcock and, when cornered at the party, she proactively handcuffs herself back to the Man, before they waltz through the party throng ('I need your love,' she now sings) and again take flight. Overall, technically and

Figure 5.1 'Hounds of Love' – 'I Don't Know What's Good for Me'.

thematically it constitutes an assured directorial debut, successfully employing allusion to create a diegetic structure and, for the connoisseur, provide a wider cultural resonance.

Bush next demonstrated that she could, if so minded, create a (literally) crowd-pleasing promo video. 'The Big Sky', released (in a 'Special Single Mix') on 28 April 1986 as *Hounds of Love*'s fourth and final single, reached number 37 in the UK. While sonically upbeat, the number offers a nostalgic lament for the simple pleasures of childhood, abandoned by many on becoming adults, such as the playful pareidolia of gazing at clouds and discerning shapes in them. As Bush sings how 'that cloud looks like Ireland', Piers Martin opines that she is 'gushing with delight, like a *Play School* presenter', referencing BBC's 1964–1988 preschool-targeted series (2022: 64).

The accompanying (4.21-minute) video, filmed over three days in late-March 1986 at Elstree Film Studios, quickly focuses on the singer, pulling back from a close-up on her eyes to Bush wearing a silver flying-suit and perched on a rooftop, observing the night sky through giant binoculars. A (potentially alienating) montage shows her standing atop a chimney in various guises, not just a firefighter, aviator and falconer, but also, accompanied by a knowing grin, figures from children's cinema, a black raincoat and umbrella connoting Julie Andrews' 'perfect nanny' from *Mary Poppins* (Robert Stevenson, 1964), while a bicorne and telescope recalls the piratical Captain Hook from the regularly referenced *Peter Pan*. On the lyric to 'jump', all becomes more grounded and dance-infused as Bush flamenco claps and shimmies through a phalanx of sky-bound travellers, World War I aviators, NASA astronauts, even Superman, film-resurgent since Richard Donner's 1978 blockbuster success. Two minutes in, Bush hits the Elstree stage, crowded with her military-clad band and GI-dressed dancers for an extended and dynamic performance piece, one that adds momentum to the song's otherwise rambling run-out. To form the crowd watching her stage choreography, Bush put out a call to her Homeground fan club: 120 lucky fans were bussed in on day two and energised the spectacle as an enthusiastic diegetic audience. The resultant video, fast-edited and lip-synched throughout, also enthused the previously wary MTV where it was frequently aired, and nominated for Best Female Video at their 1987 Video Music Awards.

However, while a popular success, this was not the overtly commercial path Bush wanted to take, and the video allows a second address. The lines complaining how 'You never understood me' and 'never really tried' can be read, amidst the song's joyful affirmations, as a barbed criticism of her record company (and/or MTV) and their advocacy she should conform to mainstream tastes. For a Bush creation, the staged dance sections are loose-looking, with the star and entourage striking unoriginal, even clichéd poses (exactly the aesthetic 'Running Up That Hill' had sought to oppose): one senses a parody of rather than compliance to expected music video tropes.

Additionally, amidst the celebratory sound and vision, a more serious mise-en-scène is discernible. Bush pointed out that, in singing of a cloud invoking Noah to '"C'mon and build me an Ark"', her composition 'is also suggesting the coming of the next flood – how perhaps the "fools on the hills" will be the wise ones' (*Kate Bush Club Newsletter*, 18, 1985). While not quite revisiting the apocalypse as portrayed in 'Breathing', this suggestion can explain the video's more threatening wartime iconography (and two giraffe costumes amidst the military throng). When jumping from the rooftops, Bush lands in a timeline of geo-political tension where various national flags fly in the background. She moves to a stage strewn with bombed rubble where the GIs re-enact Joe Rosenthal's iconic 1945 photograph of the flag-raising on Iwo Jima, while Del Palmer snarls and twirls in a Soviet officer's uniform. Even the (fan-favourite) bridge line 'And we pause for the jets' is here forebodingly matched with the silhouette of a Lancaster-style heavy bomber passing over a full moon. The graphic match where that moon becomes the spotlight for Bush and band members to perform suggests a visual parallel between music and the military, how simple pleasure is always endangered and ultimately finite. Graeme Thomson describes 'The Big Sky' as 'an almost perfect pop song, as simple or as complex as you wish it to be' (2015: 214). Bush's accompanying video can similarly be read as depicting both a song of innocence *and* experience.

Bush was determined to pursue her own visions, and her solo-work employment of Britain's moving image heritage is again evident in the video for 'Experiment IV', a low-key melodically horizontal number written as a new track for 1986's compilation album *The Whole Story*.[2] Released on 27 October 1986 as the promotional single (backed with a reworked 'Wuthering Heights'), it peaked at number 23 in the UK. The song foregrounds the martial undercurrent of 'The Big Sky' and relates a top secret military undertaking where a team of scientists, believing they are treating 'Music made for pleasure', are reassigned to create instead a sound capable of killing people at distance. Detailing how this sound includes mothers' cries and frightful screaming, the song specifies that the reluctant scientists, sworn to secrecy, hope the work will be aborted, but it ends openly, noting only that the public have been warned to stay away.

The accompanying video, conceived, produced and directed by Bush, who also briefly performs in various guises, 'fleshes out' the song, employing a longer (4.39-minute) 'Video Mix' (finally released on 2019's compilation album, *The Other Sides*) and offering a more thought-provoking conclusion. Attracting a star-filled British cast and filmed at the Royal Herbert Hospital, Greenwich, a military hospital part-designed by Florence Nightingale but abandoned since 1977, the video is set in a secret military research centre where a scientific unit is developing a deadly sound. We see the sound being created – microphones prepared for three heavily pregnant women, recording the screams of a writhing strait-jacketed 'madman' (Paddy Bush) – but also the effects of exposure to the final mix: a test-case (Del Palmer), tied to a chair, sees the sound manifest, and haemorrhages to death. The sound is given shape by Bush herself who morphs from an alluring angelic apparition into a terrifying winged demon aka banshee that kills both test-case and observing scientists. The camera assumes the demon's point of view as it escapes the lab and swoops along the centre's corridors, slaughtering all in its path, including the army general (Peter Vaughan) who (in the sole lip-synched section) authorised the experiment. A pull-back shows the research centre, fronted by a music shop and surrounded by corpses, fenced off with overhead surveillance. The demon, now Bush in civvies, hitches a lift into town.

'Experiment IV' can be adjudged a companion piece to 'Cloudbusting' with the theme of beauty/goodness being twisted into ugliness/evil. This time the experiment goes badly wrong, but the scientists are again depicted as sympathetic, manipulated by sinister figures in authority. Perhaps because single-authored, the work is more tonally assured, underlaying its horror tropes with gentle irony. This is signalled by the casting of alternative comedians Dawn French and Hugh Laurie as lab assistants, and continues with visual word play – the professor reluctantly overseeing the research (Richard Vernon) is named on secret files as Jerry Coe, punning on Jericho where, as related in the *Book of Joshua* (6: 1–27), the city walls collapsed when surrounding Israelites blew their trumpets. Bush adds an intriguing note in the final image, turning to camera and placing her index finger over her mouth. 'Shush,' she indicates, ostensibly inviting us to collude in her escape from the centre and to further slaughter. It can, though, be interpreted as a summative conclusion on the video: better to 'stay silent', its auteur-actor informs us, than turn music's creative potential into a tool of destruction. Narratively, there is a logic to the demon's acts of destruction: the scientists are killed by the very sound tools (tapes and telephones) they are (mis-)using: so too is the general, his phonecall to the centre summoning Bush, now attired as an army officer, who brings him tea, but not, it transpires, sympathy. There are accomplished set pieces: the dollied mid-shot following Professor Coe's arrival and speeded descent of the corridor is paralleled by the demon's point-of-view travelling shot back down and out of the building, a sequence reminiscent of the vast clerks pool in *Brazil* and, beyond that, the trench tracking shots of *Paths of Glory* (Stanley Kubrick, 1957).[3] Even the piece's intratextual marker coheres better than in 'Cloudbusting': the report on the army general's desk is discreetly headed *The Whole Story*.

Potentially aiding popular acceptance, the song/video's theme of sonic warfare was culturally 'in the air'. It resonated with a narrative strand in the recent space opera *Dune* (David Lynch, 1984), adapted from Frank Herbert's 1965 novel, where the Fremen employ sound weapons to repel invading Harkonnens. More parochially, and recalling the aviator iconography prevalent in 'The Big Sky', the concept also featured in the concurrent British sci-fi adventure romp *Biggles* aka *Biggles: Adventure in Time* (John Hough, 1986) where, radically reworking the books of W.E. Johns, the titular Royal Flying Corps pilot (Neil Dickson) stops Germany gaining a decisive Great War advantage by destroying their revolutionary 'sound weapon'.[4]

Pervasively postmodern, intertextuality works here at sonic, visual and generic levels. The song is punctuated by flamboyant violinist Nigel Kennedy replicating Bernard Herrmann's distinctive screeching score from the shower scene in Hitchcock's *Psycho*. Bush appearing as an angelic beauty (Figure 5.2) that flies wispily around the human

Figure 5.2 'Experiment IV' – The Sound Siren.

protagonists before transforming into a fatal demon borrows heavily from the denouement to *Raiders of the Lost Ark* (Steven Spielberg, 1981) where the ark's protective spirits shift into terrifying face-melting forms. The closing collusion with the spectator recalls another Hitchcock film, his dark comedy thriller *Family Plot* (1976), which ends with duplicitous psychic Blanche Tyler (Barbara Harris) winking at the camera.

More holistically, Alex Ramon cogently summarises 'Experiment IV' as a '*Quatermass*-meets-*The Comic Strip Presents...* sci-fi extravaganza' (2022: 99). The *Quatermass* serials, running from *The Quatermass Experiment* (BBC, 1953) to *Quatermass* (ITV, 1979), were created by Nigel Kneale, a writer frequently associated with television science fiction but who fits as readily into the horror genre, and with an emphasis here closely eliding with Bush. As Lorna Jowett and Stacey Abbott note, 'Kneale's approach to horror explores the relationship between science, technology and the supernatural, often by undermining rational foundations or highlighting the horrors of science' (2013: 94). While the various *Quatermass* iterations often have an anti-authoritarian slant, the emphasis in 'Experiment IV' on sound and spirits clashing with modern technology chimes particularly with another Kneale offering, *The Stone Tape* (BBC2, tx. 25 December 1972). Broadcast in the corporation's annual Christmas ghost story slot and directed, like 1967's *Wuthering Heights*, by Peter Sasdy, it follows a team of scientists who explore residual hauntings in the fabric of their new research centre, a renovated Victorian mansion, but release instead a malevolent and ultimately murderous presence. 'It's a mistake in the making,' as Bush sings in 'Experiment IV'.

For all its integral achievements and timely intertextual richness, the video for 'Experiment IV' was again too ambitious for its medium: as with 'Cloudbusting' it was banned from *Top of the Pops* who this time deemed it too violent for their family-friendly time slot.[5] Once more it found its UK home on cinema screens, supporting a variety of main features. It did, though, play on MTV and received a Grammy nomination for Best Concept Music Video, recognition that may have helped give Bush the confidence to direct (or co-direct) each video related to her next two albums.

In the first of these, Bush pulls back on moving image allusions. The title track and lead single for *The Sensual World* (released 18 September 1989 and reaching number 12 in the UK) was based on James Joyce's 1922 modernist novel *Ulysses*: it was not, though, film- or television-inspired like 'Wuthering Heights' – so step down Milo O'Shea and Barbara Jefford in *Ulysses* (Joseph Strick, 1967). Instead, Bush was entranced by a 1960 spoken-word album of soliloquies from the novel, specifically Molly Bloom's closing stream-of-consciousness episode (chapter 18) read by Irish actress Siobhán McKenna.[6] With the song imagining Molly stepping out of the black-and-white, two-dimensional pages of the novel into the real world with all its new pleasures to experience (and away from its male author since, with permission refused by Joyce's estate, Bush had to paraphrase the soliloquy), its accompanying video, where Bush dances – with apposite female empowerment and sensuality – through an enchanted forest in long velvet medieval dress and veiled hat, was co-directed with *The Comic Strip Presents*' Peter Richardson.[7]

The motivation for composing 'This Woman's Work' has been discussed (Chapter 3). For its (UK number 25) single release on 20 November 1989, Bush directed a fresh music video with a theme similar to the song's placement in *She's Having a Baby*, here with *Les Dogs*' Tim McInnerny pacing a hospital waiting room and recalling happier times as he awaits news on his wife (Bush), who collapsed as they were having dinner. The Bush-directed video to accompany the album's third and final single, 'Love and Anger' (released 26 February 1990 and reaching number 35 in the UK), was essentially a straight performance piece, with the initially spotlit singer in a black dress joined first by white-clad choruses of ballet dancers then whirling dervishes, who appear (provocatively) just as she sings of 'the priest' – potentially indicating (unlike on the message-jettisoning video to 'Them Heavy People') the many paths to 'a heaven inside'. Mostly, though, she is joined by the KT Bush Band with Pink Floyd's Richard Wright on keyboard and Dave Gilmour on lead guitar, complete with (standard rock video) wind machine. Like the song itself, it seems to show Bush losing aesthetic momentum.

More allusive (and visually intriguing), in 1989 Bush also recorded a reggae-inflected cover version of the 1972 hit 'Rocket Man', her contribution to the Elton John–Bernie Taupin tribute album *Two Rooms*. This became a number 2 hit in Australia and UK number 12 when (backed with her recording of the duo's 'Candle in the Wind') it enjoyed a single release on 25 November 1991.[8] Her version was accompanied by a Bush-directed black-and-white promo video. Again mostly a performance piece with her band, this time, with a gesture to the connoisseur, Bush's shimmies and ukulele strumming present a homage to Marilyn Monroe playing Sugar 'Kane' Kowalczyk in *Some Like It Hot* (Billy Wilder, 1959). Additionally, a brief section where Bush in close-up dons a space helmet potentially references the gender role-challenging Ellen Ripley (Sigourney Weaver) in *Alien*, but also recalls 'Starman' David Bowie and his initial rendition of 'Space Oddity', recorded for his promotional film *Love You Till Tuesday* (Malcolm J. Thompson, 1969) and given a high-profile VHS release in May 1984 (Figure 5.3). The image cutting in as

72 *Video*

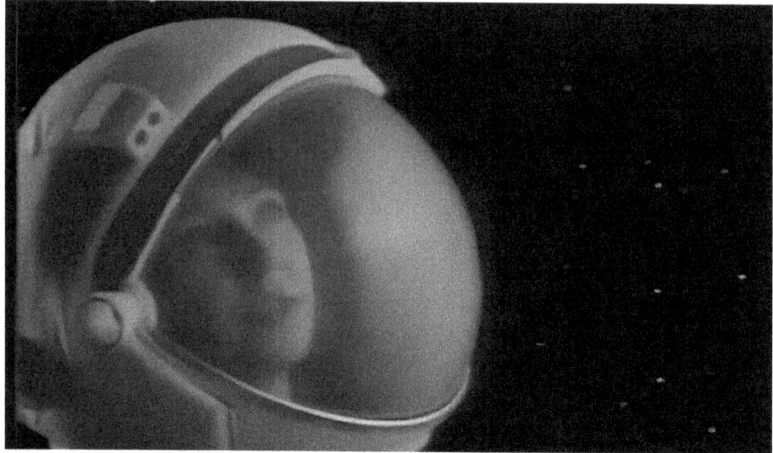

Figure 5.3 'Rocket Man' – Bush meets Bowie.

Bush sings how 'Mars ain't the kind of place to raise your kids' adds a further intertextuality, chiming with Bowie's own 1971 questioning of 'Life of Mars?'.⁹

'Rocket Man' partially plugged a four-year gap until Bush's sole album release of the 1990s, the deeply film-influenced *The Red Shoes* (examined in Chapter 6). This was followed by a further 12-year hiatus in Bush's career (spent raising her son Bertie).¹⁰ Perhaps absence made the heart grow fonder since the double-album *Aerial*, released on 7 November 2005, was critically eulogised and reached number 3 in the UK charts and 48 on the US Billboard 200. For Christopher Knowles 'a postmodern pagan liturgy to the sky and sea' (2010: 123), it was, like *Hounds of Love*, divided into two distinct thematic sections. The second half, subtitled 'A Sky of Honey', was a single piece treating outside experiences across a summer's day. The first section, subtitled 'A Sea of Honey' and more disparate in nature, included the outlier track 6, 'Joanni', a hymn to female empowerment which, describing epic battle scenes and Joan of Arc 'so beautiful in her armour', could evoke actor-supermodel Milla Jovovich's recent defiantly modern portrayal in *The Messenger: The Story of Joan of Arc / Jeanne d'Arc* (Luc Besson, 1999).

This section also includes the album's sole single release, track 1, 'King of the Mountain'. Released on 24 October 2005, it peaked at number 4 on its UK chart entry. The song reflects on the pressures of wealth and fame but, like 'Get Out of My House', its expression, while feasibly earthed in personal experience, again becomes that 'strange mixture' typical of Bush for being filtered through a cultural construct.

Here Bush combines figures from music and movies as she wonders whether Elvis Presley aka the King of Rock and Roll (1935–1977(?)) might have faked his death and still be living somewhere incognito, happily playing 'in the snow with Rosebud', the childhood sleigh of the increasingly reclusive title character of the celebrated *Citizen Kane* (Orson Welles, 1941).

This time the accompanying video was entrusted to American director/animator Jimmy Murakami. Nonetheless, there were lengthy collaborations with Bush (who vetoed 3D computer work) on narrative and storyboarding that helped Murakami to achieve an effective visual correlation for the song's comparison of what, in interview, Bush termed Kane and the King's 'unbearable fame' (John Wilson, *Front Row*, BBC Radio 4, 4 November 2005). The video opens, as newspaper headlines regarding Elvis swirl by, with a black-and-white rerun of the exposition to *Citizen Kane* and a series of 'aerial' shots passing through Charles Foster Kane (Welles)'s art-laden Gothic mansion Xanadu, windswept and cavernous until Bush appears and, with a deep Elvis drawl, questions why a multi-millionaire should fill his home with 'priceless junk'. It closes with a return to Kane's 'stately pleasure-dome' and, as in Welles' film, a close-up on the sleigh with 'Rosebud' written across it.

Though Bush sways elegantly in a bulky brown overcoat, the dance moves, like the promo's direction, are entrusted elsewhere, here to a live-animated white Elvis jumpsuit, bell-bottomed and rhinestone-encrusted with matching belt and cape, a synecdoche for the aging star since worn on the worldwide satellite-beamed television special *Elvis: Aloha From Hawaii* (Marty Pasetta, 1973). Despite its ineluctable associations with Elvis, the mining of Bush's own film experience is (for the connoisseur) also evident in two brief scenes, first where Bush's dance with the jumpsuit replicates Moira Shearer dancing with an animated newspaper in *The Red Shoes* (see Chapter 7), and again when the suit takes wing with a skein of Canada geese, just like Yasha Mazur at the end of *The Magician of Lublin*, the film where Bush made her first soundtrack contribution.[11] Reuniting the song's explicit twin cultural referents, the suit flies to the Himalayas ('Sightings of Elvis in Yeti Colony', reads the headline on a mocked-up *Ohio Chronicle*) where it meets up with an elderly and bearded Elvis in his mountain hideaway, sleigh-riding like young Kane. As Graeme Thomson adjudged, 'It was a good video, both funny and poignant' (2015: 305).

After *Aerial* a further wait ensued for 'new' material. Long unhappy at the sound of her sixth and seventh studio albums, feeling that pressure to use the latest digital tape and fill the new CD format had betrayed her original ambitions, on 16 May 2011 Bush released a revision of four tracks from *The Sensual World* and seven from *The Red Shoes*. In the spirit of film directors dissatisfied with original prints, she called the reworked album *Director's Cut*. The first release on her own Fish People record label, the cinematic concept for this analogue 'take two' continued on the album's artwork, its front cover showing Bush with scissors inspecting a length of celluloid, while inside the surrealistic shots from photographer Tim Walker suggested, for Rob Young, 'the interiorised filmic spaces of a [Jean] Cocteau, [David] Lynch or the ritualistic scenes of Kubrick's *Eyes Wide Shut* [1999]' (2022: 101).

Three numbers, 'This Woman's Work', 'Rubberband Girl' and 'Moments of Pleasure', were completely re-recorded, while the other tracks contained new lead vocals, plus remixes that repatched, overdubbed and often added new musicians. With permission finally granted to quote James Joyce verbatim, 'The Sensual World' received new lyrics, a (frankly underwhelming) new mix, and a new title, 'Flower of the Mountain'. It was not, though, the recipient of a new music video. Instead, the album's lead single became the reworked track 4, 'Deeper Understanding': released as a digital download on 5 April 2011, it reached 87 in the UK singles chart. Telling of the disillusioned narrator's growing relationship with their computer, the song was premonitory on *The Sensual World*, but now felt fully on trend. Also, where the original had deployed a basic vocoder to distort the chorus but needed untreated backing vocals from the female ensemble Trio Bulgarka to render the lyrics discernible, thus compromising the intended human–machine interaction, studio advances meant that the reworked version, now two minutes longer (6.33), could employ the originally desired single siren-like computerised voice, here manipulated from Bush's son Bertie. The added harmonica solo may drag but, as Sasha Frere-Jones noted, 'Where the original chattered and cracked, this version susurrates and warps, a bit more like life online' ('The Bush Doctrine', *New Yorker*, 30 May 2011).

The promo video, with Bush resuming direction but for the first time staying behind the camera, returned to the 'small film' format and featured fellow *Comic Strip* regular Robbie Coltrane as a businessman who becomes so fixated with the new 'Voice Console' programme he has uploaded to his computer that his wife (Frances Barber) leaves him and takes with her their two children. His new 'relationship' does not prosper, though: when the Console, having sent out entrancing multicoloured sound waves, seemingly malfunctions, it makes Coltrane's character hallucinate uncomfortably about the mockery of friends and family. When it then escapes out the window as a ball of light, the besotted businessman follows it through the streets to find another addict (Bush parodist Noel Fielding) enjoying 'his' Console and, in jealousy, strangles him.

Warning of the anti-social tendencies inherent in modern technology (and like 'Experiment IV' its potential to infect entire populations), the video again chimes with surrounding film projects. Presenting the Voice Console as just a pair of red lips filling the white screen (Figure 5.4) most evidently resonates with Debbie Harry's immersive 'breathing screen' seductress Nicki Brand in *Videodrome* (David Cronenberg, 1983), a film that, for postmodern guru Fredric Jameson (and with discourse redolent of Wilhelm Reich), 'triumphantly evades all high cultural qualities, from technical perfection to the discrimination of taste and the orgonon of beauty' (1992: 22). For this viewer, and indicative of a late move towards more minimalist expression, the disembodied lips also offer a recontextualisation of Samuel Beckett's 14-minute dramatic – and traumatic – stream-of-consciousness monologue *Not I* (1972), distinctly high culture and filmed in 2000 by Neil Jordan with Julianne Moore as the screen-filling mouth. Looking back, a visual link can also be offered to the early animations of mentor Terry Gilliam, Paul Wells noting that 'One of the most interesting images' in his work, 'perhaps referencing Beckett's *Not I* ... is a man's mouth that detaches itself from the banality of the presenter speaking through it' (2020: 96). Looking forward, and again indicative of the work's prescience, its narrative conceit closely anticipates *Her* (Spike Jonze, 2013) where introverted Theodore Twombly (Joaquin Phoenix) develops a 'relationship' with his new operating system's AI

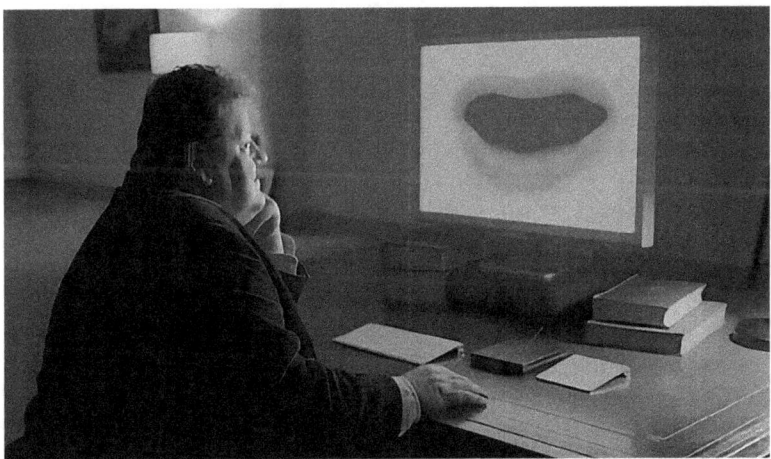

Figure 5.4 'Deeper Understanding' – Bush meets Beckett.

virtual assistant, the female-voiced Samantha (Scarlett Johansson). Peter Marks terms *Her* a film with 'a disturbing subtext' where the materially utopian existence of its characters is 'complicated by technological advances, social atomisation, and the tensions between traditional and emerging gender roles, where real and virtual worlds are in a transitional state' (2019: 141). It is a description equally fitting for Bush's music video.

Having grown accustomed to waiting several years between Bush album releases, two came along in quick succession. On 21 November 2011, just six months after *Director's Cut*, Bush released her tenth studio album, *50 Words for Snow* – it debuted and peaked at number 5 in the UK album charts, and at 83 on the Billboard 200. Bush again left behind her tightly crafted, studio-layered short song format, foregrounding instead her piano playing for seven longer stripped-back and meditative pieces, although, as Ann Powers observes, 'still she gives us something cinematic, all reflecting a central theme', here the notion of falling snow and the wider significance of winter (2022).

By now the standing of the pop music video had changed, proliferating over social platforms but thereby sacrificing a central focus – Will Straw termed the medium now 'both ubiquitous and minor' (2018: 187). The era of highly financed and glossily produced videos as a key promotional vehicle via television music channels had largely passed and so, to promote the album's release, Bush explored fresh visual terrain, and a trio of low-budget artisanal animations, each different in style and manufacture, were released exclusively online. Early Gilliam is again pertinent: Wells notes how his seemingly child-focused cartoonal work also 'speaks to adult audiences through the "naïveté" of the animated form', and Bush's animations offer a similar dual address, engaging with the form 'only to "smuggle" in more complex issues' (2004: 124).

The advance single, track 4's (7.17-minute) 'Wild Man', recounts over Eastern keyboard motifs the efforts made to protect the (unnamed) Yeti aka 'Kangchenjunga Demon, Wild Man, Metoh-Kangmi' from discovery in the wilds of the Himalayas: released as a digital download on 11 October 2011, it reached 73 on the UK charts. For album rather than single stimulus, a 2.33-minute 'Animation Segment' of the song, covering its chorus and final verse where she entreats tolerance for those 'othered' like the Yeti, was posted on 16 November both on Bush's official website and YouTube. Directed by Bush and created by Finn and Patrick at Brandt Animation, the video, revisiting terrain covered in 'King of the Mountain' but now accepting of imaging software, featured Bush, in close-up and wrapped in (faux) furs against the icy conditions, digitally treated to integrate with CGI animations of expeditionary forces, shadowy mountain presences and the ubiquitous snowfall (Figure 5.5).

Figure 5.5 'Wild Man' – Bush meets Yeti Hunters.

Snow in animation regularly constitutes a space of enchantment but here an invasive rhetoric is emphasised. The piece thus resonates with another Hammer horror, the Nigel Kneale-scripted *The Abominable Snowman* (Val Guest, 1957), similar for its pro-Yeti stance, the final sighting only of the Yeti's eyes, and its widescreen monochrome vistas yet 'taut, paranoid atmosphere' (Hearn and Barnes 2007: 27). The medium is especially effective for 'Wild Man' since, as Annabelle Honess Roe notes, animation can treat concepts and subjectivities difficult to represent in live action imagery and, by employing 'an abstract or symbolic style', functions 'as an aide imagination that can facilitate awareness, understanding and compassion from the audience for a subject position far removed from its own' (2013: 25).

Two further animated segments, also written-directed by Bush, were sequentially released, again on her own digital platform and YouTube. These now showcased crafted handmade techniques, a process particularly associated in animation studies with what Wells terms 'a specifically *feminine aesthetic* which resists the inherently masculine language of the live-action arena, and the most dominant codes of orthodox hyper-realist animation which also uses its vocabulary' (1998: 198). A 2.24-minute section of track 3, 'Misty', entitled 'Mistraldespair' and created for Bush by Tommy Thompson and Gary Pureton, was released on 25 November 2011. This offered a stop-motion claymated variant on Dianne Jackson (and Jimmy Murakami)'s animated film *The Snowman* (Channel 4, tx. 26 December 1982), based on Raymond Briggs' 1978 picture book, and was equally poignant in its depiction of the fleeting relationship between human and snowman, but distinctly more adult in tone. The album track, delivered by Bush with a quiet and breathy vocal, is a 13.32-minute love song from a woman to a snowman who, 'after their one and only tryst', by morning has melted away, leaving only dead leaves and branches. Readable as a metaphor for ephemeral or even frigid love affairs, Bush clarified in interview with John Doran the scenario's reality, for her at least, and how 'in that particular song obviously there is a sexual encounter going on' ('A Demon in the Drift: Kate Bush Interviewed', *The Quietus*, 21 March 2014) – which adds another level of significance to lyrics describing wet bedsheets and melting in the woman's hands. In Bush's video, covering the final verse (where the snowman dissolves) and building on the album cover's ice-carved representation of a snowman whose puckered lips touch those of a young woman, we witness a more chaste encounter (Aardman before 'hard' man, perhaps). Here the emphasis is on caresses and hands being held by the woman (strongly resembling Bush herself) and the snowman who has entered through her bedroom window, the couple lying together until, unlike the abrupt and abrasive ending to *The Snowman*, he slowly melts in her arms, leaving her holding just his head.

The album's third and most achieved animation dropped on 24 January 2012. 'Eider Falls at Lake Tahoe' is a companion to track 2, the 11.08-minute 'Lake Tahoe' where, to stripped-back percussion and piano, Bush relates the tale of a woman who, in Victorian times, fell into Sierra Nevada's titular 'cold mountain water' and whose ghost still occasionally appears, calling to her dog Snowflake.[12] The accompanying video, running at 5.01 minutes and following the dog on its long journey over land and sea back to its lakeside home, is a black-and-white shadow puppet animation in the style of pioneer German director Lotte Reiniger and her feature film *The Adventures of Prince Achmed / Die Abenteuer des Prinzen Achmed* (1926). Reiniger's style is again, for Wells, distinctly feminine due to 'the lyrical movement of the figures, and the emotional intensity of *gesture* – a profound departure from the (male) agendas of the evolving cartoon' (1998: 201). For Bush's animation, the puppets were designed by Robert Allsopp and filmed by another of Gilliam's long-time collaborators (beginning as director of photography on *Brazil*), Academy Award nominee Roger Pratt. Pratt had worked on the second and fourth Harry Potter films, though not *Harry Potter and the Deathly Hallows: Part 1* (David Yates, 2010) where, as Hermione Grainger (Emma Watson) narrates the magical 'Tale of the Three Brothers', the film shifts to a beguiling 3-minute sequence of sepia-toned shadow puppetry (designed-directed by Ben Hibon with Framestore led by Dale Newton). Alongside Reiniger's oldest surviving animated feature, one can conjecture the influence of this recent much-admired sequence on Bush's own elegant, 'feminine', and supernatural animation, one where the medium is temporally appropriate to the subject matter since 'optical "toys"' such as shadow puppets and silhouettes are generally accepted as popular Victorian 'precursors of cinema' (Sergeant 2005: 11). Elegiac in tone, the song is also thematically appropriate to Bush's career: the nineteenth-century female ghost effecting a final-verse reunion with her beloved ('good boy / You've come home') can be read as constituting an older, more lyrical and intensely *gestured* variant on the narrative impulse of her debut hit 'Wuthering Heights'.

A more explicit revisiting/reworking of Bush's back catalogue leads to one further and (to date) final video production. Almost 30 years after its release, Bush recorded a video for 'And Dream of Sheep', the opening section of *Hounds of Love*'s 'The Ninth Wave'. It was shot principally to be shown during her 'Before the Dawn' shows in late-summer 2014. Here Bush, who sings live rather than lip-synching, appears floating in moonlit water, strapped to a lifejacket with its emergency beacon blinking on her left side like a fragile heartbeat and, when not struggling to retain consciousness, looking up at the camera with expressions readable as ranging from determination to supplication to resignation (Figure 5.6). The 3.40-minute piece, helmed by rehired David Garfath, was shot over three days at Pinewood Studios in a special water tank – the search for realism led, apparently, to Bush, in method acting style, catching mild hypothermia after spending too long in the tank on the first day (*Guardian*, 21 November 2016). Each evening of the residency, beginning Part Two, the Hammersmith curtain opened to show, projected on a high-hanging oval

Figure 5.6 'And Dream of Sheep (Live)' – A Late Resurfacing.

screen, the short film of Bush shipwrecked and at sea, singing of her 'Little light shining'. She thus becomes a (literally) 'disembodied presence', as Pete Paphides' review noted, 'all but unreachable to the singers who impassively assume the role of Greek chorus to her plight' (*Hidden Tracks*, 28 August 2014).[13] Just over two years later, on 18 November 2016, the video dropped alongside 'And Dream of Sheep (Live)', the promotional single release for the *Before the Dawn* box-set, a three-part live album covering the show and credited to the KT Fellowship: released a week after the video, the album reached number 4 on the UK's album chart and was certified Gold (100,000-plus unit sales).[14]

This prompts a broader retrospective. Much has been made (rightly) of Bush's rediscovery via 'Running Up That Hill', charting again after 37 years and exemplifying how a single work of art can, over time, be repurposed and elicit fresh meanings. It can be equally fruitful to bracket the works of a single artist over a career and, as Bush's latest video, 'And Dream of Sleep (Live)' (like 'Lake Tahoe') repays comparison and contrast with her video debut, the Keith MacMillan-directed 'Wuthering Heights', released 38 years earlier. Across the decades one can detect a unity of cadre and construction in the two pieces. With no distracting background decor, both videos focus solely on the charismatic singer, the later fuller of face but instantly recognisable with the same distinctive lips, long auburn hair and mesmeric star presence. Both videos project songs written by Bush and performed by her as personae in elegiac mode and liminal states, initially singing as a woman returning from the dead and asking to be let in, finally as a woman in fear of imminent death and hoping to be pulled out.

Significant differences are equally apparent, however, revelatory of the later maturity of performer and performance. 'Wuthering Heights' is, of course, a young woman's work, exciting in its kinetic energy and high-pitched voice redolent of teenage angst, but almost frantic in its stylised movements and image duplication. By contrast, 'And Dream of Sheep (Live)' is still, almost inactive. Entirely exempt from accusations of 'the eccentric displays of amateur dramatics' heaped on the ingenue, her later work is, I would contend, again reminiscent of the disciplined dramaturgy of Samuel Beckett (especially with its initial site-specific staging). Bush performs 'And Dream of Sleep (Live)' as a watery variant on Winnie from Beckett's *Happy Days* (1961), an older woman who, buried in the earth and sinking up to her neck, parallels 'The Ninth Wave' by intoning with rhythm, repetition and temporal jumps what Fiona Shaw has called her 'self-preservatory illusions' (2008: 111).[15]

'You are changeless' Winnie tells herself (Beckett 1990: 165): the judgement is both true and not true, as it is for Bush. From 'Wuthering

Heights' onwards, Bush's music videos have consistently pushed at the boundaries of the medium, risking ridicule (or refusal) while expanding it beyond commercial expediency into authentic artistic expression, initially with mentor assistance, later with auteur autonomy. Her final pieces have continued the artistic quest, retreating from interpretative dance (age here undoubtedly a factor) while exponentially exploring the potentialities of animation and CGI until, finally, (explicit) Brontë shifts to (implicit) Beckett. Anna McMullan argues that *Happy Days*, in text and staging, 'draws attention to the limits of the visible, what is hidden, withheld, unseeable, or unreadable from the audience's perspective' (2010: 55). Bush too, in her latest video, continues to interrogate the feasible: exploring the epistemological dimensions of the moving image, pushing at the unreadable and unreachable, she presents her minimalist video of the absurd, daringly taking us 'deeper and deeper'.

Between these career-bracketing productions lies further experimentation. *Before the Dawn*, like the Hammersmith Apollo residency, opened with Bush's composition 'Lily'. This was originally released on *The Red Shoes* album, chronologically a near mid-point between 'Wuthering Heights' and 'And Dream of Sleep (Live)'. Given that, amidst her myriad film and television allusions, Ron Moy denotes *The Red Shoes* as 'the artist's most high-profile and direct homage to a prior text' (2007: 114), it merits extended and discrete analysis. This is undertaken in Part 3's detailed case study.

Notes

1 In interview Bush agreed with Maria Montgomery Sarnoff that her 'early videos are more staged' and 'theatrically and dance-influenced', but averred they 'are more film-influenced now' ('Perfect Vision', *Option*, March 1990).
2 Given Bush's employment of personae, Hitchcock's *Psycho* can be conjectured as an influence on the album title. At the film's conclusion, psychiatrist Dr Richmond (Simon Oakland) explains Norman's alternate personality: 'I got the whole story, but not from Norman. I got it from his mother. Norman Bates no longer exists.'
3 The demonic point-of-view shot may have been expedient: surviving rushes intimate further monstrous imagery was intended but, under time pressure from EMI to complete the video, its more ambitious post-production work was shelved.
4 On the theme of fatal sounds, a 'shout out' is merited for *The Shout* (Jerzy Skolimowski, 1978) where Alan Bates' travelling man claims to possess a shout that can kill. Given Bush's love for *Monty Python*, mention is also due to their first episode's 'Funniest Joke in the World' sketch (featuring Graham Chapman's Colonel) where anyone hearing the joke literally dies laughing (BBC1, tx. 5 October 1969).

5 Airplay preference was again accorded to a tamer staged performance (with Nigel Kennedy guesting) given on BBC1's *Wogan* (tx. 31 October 1986).
6 *James Joyce – Ulysses: Soliloquies of Molly and Leopold Bloom* – Read by Siobhán McKenna and E. G. Marshall, Caedmon Records TC 1068 (1960).
7 The song features prominently, effectively conveying the lead (Elaine Cassidy)'s isolation, in *Felicia's Journey* (Atom Egoyan, 1999).
8 Indicative of Bush's continued dividing of opinion, English indie pop group St. Etienne declared that Bush's 'Rocket Man' 'made them want to vomit' (Thomson 2015: 250); by contrast, her version topped a 2007 UK readers' poll of 'The Top 50 Greatest Covers' (*Observer Music Monthly*, 19 August 2007).
9 Sporadically broadcast at the time, the 'Rocket Man' promo only received an official release to mark *The Other Sides* box-set's dropping on 8 March 2019.
10 This absence became the subject of a 53-minute Dutch documentary film, *Come Back Kate* (Quirine Racké, Helena Muskens, 2007), which explored the lives (and theories) of a series of committed Bush fans.
11 This concept also informs her 2014 Hammersmith performances of 'Aerial' where Bush mutates into a bird and takes flight before the lights cut.
12 Not originally a single, a 10" picture disc of 'Lake Tahoe', limited to 2,000 copies and featuring the video's shadow puppets, was released to support the fifth annual Record Store Day on 21 April 2012.
13 This stage showing followed another (2.38-minute) film, 'The Astronomer's Tale', written by Bush with novelist David Mitchell. Projected on the closed curtain, the amateur astronomer (Kevin Doyle)'s explanation of picking up a sinking ship's distress signal functioned both as exposition for 'The Ninth Wave' and a stop-gap as the stage was reset for Part Two.
14 Garfath reputedly filmed Bush's 'Before the Dawn' concert in full, though (as of March 2024) this has not been released.
15 Beckett's play was filmed with Rosaleen Linehan as Winnie in *Happy Days* (Patricia Rozema, 2001).

Part 3
Film

6 A Matter of Life and Death
Kate Bush and *The Red Shoes*

Like Winnie's self-appraisal in *Happy Days*, Ron Moy's declaration that *The Red Shoes* is Kate Bush's most direct homage to a prior text is both true and not true. The claim holds at the level of album title – though the subsequent *Aerial* with its focus on domesticity and motherhood also acknowledges Sylvia Plath's posthumously published poetry volume *Ariel* (1965). However, while permeated by the Powell–Pressburger film, *The Red Shoes* is also by far Bush's most directly voiced statement of personal experience, (like Plath) building rarefied psychic landscapes and ruminating on death. The biographical background is thus uniquely important to an understanding and evaluation of this phase in the artist's career.

It took four years for Kate Bush to release her follow-up album to *The Sensual World*. While not by now an atypical wait, the contributing circumstances were uniquely traumatic. During the later sessions for *The Red Shoes*, Bush's 15-year romance with Del Palmer came to an end (though they continued to work together). Alongside this, on 14 February 1992, not long after the death of Bush's aunt Maureen, her mother, Hannah (née Daly), passed away from cancer, aged 73. A staff nurse who, with husband Robert, encouraged Kate's childhood spirit of invention, Hannah had proven an anchor of normality amidst the vagaries of international stardom, and a year after her passing the family was still, brother Paddy admitted, 'knocked sideways' (cited in Hasted 2022: 90).

This was the culmination of a succession of heartfelt losses for Bush. Lighting director Bill Duffield had fallen to his death on 2 April 1979 after a Dorset 'Tour of Life' dress-rehearsal (and became the dedicatee of 'Blow Away (for Bill)' on *Never for Ever*); Abbey Road sound engineer John Barratt (nicknamed Teddy),[1] who worked on *Never for Ever* and *The Dreaming*, died of cancer in February 1984; dance partner Gary Hurst (nicknamed Bubba – and featured in the 'There Goes a Tenner' video) died of AIDS in 1990, as had band guitarist Alan

DOI: 10.4324/9781003479604-9

Murphy in October 1989. Loss was clearly on Bush's mind, and Maureen, Bill, Teddy, Bubba and 'Murph' are all namechecked in the coda to the album track 'Moments of Pleasure'.

Film, though, remains important. A final entry in the song's litany for the faithful departed, asking 'Michael / Did you really love me?', references a more recent friendship, struck up with an elderly director Bush had long admired, British cinema luminary Michael Powell (1905–1990). In a career stretching from silent cinema to slasher movies, Powell's apprenticeship included late-1920s stills photography for Hitchcock, directing 23 'quota quickies' in the 1930s, joining with Hungarian émigré writer Emeric Pressburger for a series of war films, then together in 1942 creating the Archers production company to make films under the Rank Organisation's umbrella. The Archers period saw the apex of Powell's filmography: sharing writer-director-producer credits (though Powell directed), and with a regular cast and crew, Powell and Pressburger enjoyed a run of acclaimed success. In an age largely upholding the tenets of realism, they made a set of lavish, (mostly) technicolour fantasies with daringly experimental cinematography, namely *The Life and Death of Colonel Blimp* (1943), *A Canterbury Tale* (1944), *I Know Where I'm Going!* (1945), *A Matter of Life and Death* (1946), *Black Narcissus* (1947), *The Red Shoes* (1948), *Gone to Earth* (1950) and *The Tales of Hoffmann* (1951). As Alan Burton and Steve Chibnall note, based on these acknowledged masterpieces, 'The Archers are now internationally acclaimed as singular artists of film whose visionary work stands among the best of English-language cinema in the studio period' (2013: 40).

And their particular appeal to Bush? Andrew Moor notes Powell and Pressburger's willingness to 'transgress generic boundaries', to 'press the theme of performativity' and to question 'our ability to reinvent ourselves', which all 'equate with debates about modernity and postmodernity' (2005: 13): all are explorations in accord with Bush's working practice. In addition, their films provided prominent roles for women, often exploring the pressures placed on their female leads to conform to specific social groupings: one can understand their existential appeal to a young woman battling the patriarchal structures of the music (and associated creative) industries.

Historically, however, the Archers' acclaim did not last. With fewer successes across the 1950s, Powell and Pressburger split (amicably) in 1957 to pursue individual projects. The opprobrium Powell received for his psychological horror film *Peeping Tom* (1960) forced him to decamp to Australia where he eked out a living mostly in television: a brief low-key reunion with Pressburger preceded retirement in the Cotswolds (Christie 1994: 84–92). Reappraisal (thankfully) came in his life-time, principally due to the praise – and advisory positions – heaped on him from the late-1970s by New Hollywood directors including Martin Scorsese and Francis Ford Coppola, and in 1981 Powell received, with Pressburgur, BAFTA's highest honour, its Academy Fellowship Award.

The recognition of – and desire to work with – Powell by a younger generation of creatives came not just from America. With her thoughts turning towards visual accompaniments for her new musical projects, Bush wrote to Powell asking if he would be interested in working with her. He asked to hear her music and so she sent him a set of cassettes: this prompted an exchange of letters and a growing friendship (Jovanovic 2005: 192). In late-spring 1989, while in New York to discuss *The Sensual World*'s American release, Bush arranged to meet Powell at 44th Street's Royalton Hotel, during an unseasonal blizzard. Bush spoke fondly of their encounter in interview with Marianne Jensson:

> As we came out of the lift, [Powell] was standing outside with his walking stick and he was pretending be someone like Douglas Fairbanks. He was completely adorable and just the most beautiful spirit, and it was a very profound experience for me.
>
> ('Rubber Souls', *Vox*, November 1993)

The prospect of a collaboration did not materialise, however: Powell, already frail, died at his Gloucestershire home on 19 February 1990. Nonetheless, their Manhattan meeting is recounted in the second verse of 'Moments of Pleasure', including the comparison to Fairbanks (1883–1939), famed for swashbuckling film roles as in *The Thief of Bagdad* (Raoul Walsh, 1924), whose 1940 British remake was part-directed by Powell. That sword-swinging simile notwithstanding, Powell's appearance in the song is a rare instance to date of Bush communicating directly, eschewing the filtering of feeling through an elaborate construction of culture-derived personae. It would prove, for good or ill, a feature of *The Red Shoes*.

These personal tragedies were leading to repeated delays in the album's creation. Murphy died not long after Bush's meeting with Powell, and the deep grief his (and Hurst's) death occasioned caused Bush to stop all work for six months. During this hiatus, she may have noted the example of David Bowie who, seeking to revitalise his career, had gone back to basics by creating the four-piece band Tin Machine, active with two albums and low-key touring between 1988 and 1992. Memories of Bush's 'Tour of Life' burn-out may also have receded and, on returning to the studio, she considered resuming touring, a prospect even shared with an overjoyed fan convention (Jovanovic 2005: 184). Thus, the album's early phase emphasised a simpler 'live' sound that, stylistically eclectic and shorn of studio dependency, could be reproduced on stage.

Militating against this, Bush then made two major changes from her creative custom and practice. The first was in personnel. While the hole left by Murphy would eventually be filled by Danny McIntosh (future partner and father of Bertie), Bush initially invited a roster of 'A'-list guitarists to provide cameo performances. A 'guest star' casting including Eric Clapton, Jeff Beck and Prince would have its drawbacks, however, removing the compact reproducible sound of a live band, and entering mainstream motifs at variance with Bush's singular lyrical and sonic universe, notably overlaying her female-centred narratives with distinctly masculine musical signatures.

The second change was in production where Bush, in accord with industry advances, agreed to record the album digitally, a process she would later regret for creating what she considered a cold and tinny soundscape. This also worked against the initially desired live sound, with the greater ease of multi-tracking and pressure to fill the longer CD format arguably favouring an aesthetic of quantity before quality. Life and loss also loosened her usual authoritative studio presence. The death of Bush's mother again postponed recording – 'I couldn't work for months,' she admitted (*Vox*, November 1993) – and when sessions resumed she seemingly lacked full commitment. Palmer, who oversaw the album's mixing while Bush undertook dance lessons in preparation for *TLTC&TC*, later conceded his surprise when Bush signed off on the first offered set of mastertapes. This constituted, as Nick Hasted notes, 'a previously unthinkable lack of perfectionism' (2022: 93).

For all the difficulties in its creation (and a further two-month release delay to allow the completion of *TLTC&TC*), *The Red Shoes*, issued on 2 November 1993, succeeded both commercially and critically. The album reached second position in the UK album charts, a platinum disc indicating sales of over 300,000; it also hit number 28 on the Billboard chart, Bush's best US position to date. Press reviews were positive on both sides of the Atlantic, several fulsome in their praise. In Britain, where her Fairlight innovations and lyrical complexity had transformed Bush into the darling of the rock press, Chris Roberts declared that '*The Red Shoes* dances so far ahead of the rest it's embarrassing' and deemed the album 'An utter masterpiece' (*Melody Maker*, 30 October 1993). In America, which overlooked Bush's previous two albums, Paul Verna summarised that here the 'Alternative rock icon throws a sumptuous feast of sounds that is destined to take a high place in her body of work' (*Billboard*, 27 November 1993: 98). In retrospect, such effusive reviews strike as generous – *The Red Shoes* is now generally adjudged a lesser entry in the Bush canon. Graeme Thomson postulates that many critics fell into the trap of wishful listening, 'expressing a laudable sentiment at precisely the wrong time', and argues that the album proves that the confessional mode was not Bush's 'natural gift'. Instead, 'Spelling out what she was once able to suggest and imply ... for once she failed to make glorious artifice out of her art. She does not transcend' (2015: 258–259).

Again, this is both true and not true. Though this is not a musicological study, it is beneficial briefly to examine the tracks on *The Red Shoes*. First, a dialectic exploration offers evidence (including via absence) of how the use of musical allusion allows Bush a more achieved shaping of personal experiences, and conversely how, without the structuring conduit and thematic resonance of references to pre-existing works, her writing can, as on occasions here, become musically indifferent and lyrically indecipherable. The two tiers of reception outlined by Noël Carroll, where allusion offers knowing 'connoisseurs' further appreciation while unknowing 'consumers' can still enjoy the work, risk collapsing when that work evidently functions like a *chanson à clef*, but one to which the listener frustratingly has no key: Andy Gill's album review, for instance, found that the 'private lyric' on 'Moments of Pleasure' with its 'impenetrable references ... renders the song too solipsistic to transmit beyond her immediate circle' (*Q*, 86, November 1993). Nonetheless, in (partial) counterargument this investigation will show how *The Red Shoes* does not lack accessible allusion, notably to film, which extends beyond the title track. Second, and more fully pertinent to this study's third part, the songs necessitate exegesis since their themes and tone feed directly into Bush's related film production, *TLTC&TC* (examined in Chapter 7).

Much like Powell and Pressburger's cinematic creations, Bush's album aims for an imaginative myth-invested production, and it particularly echoes the Archers' version of *The Red Shoes* with its ambiguous presentation of the tensions between commitment to art and the private life. The importance of the title track, and its film-associated themes, is apparent from the album artwork, Bush's first long-play release not to feature her image on the front cover. Instead, it carries a picture of two feet wearing the titular red satin ballet shoes (plus laddered tights), one foot *en pointe* resting in a small pool of blood, all against a background of crashing waves plus brooding clouds, and encased in a circular black border. A fetishizing image that will also feature in *TLTC&TC*, it recalls the statuette of a ballet-slippered foot in the Powell–Pressburger film fondled by impresario Lermontov as he recounts the original Hans Christian Andersen tale, complete with his throwaway summary of its denouement – 'Oh, in the end she dies'.

The back cover lists the song titles over a cornucopia of fruit, while the inner sleeve houses the printed lyrics, backed by further fruit, now sliced open, and a black-and-white image of Bush leaning back but held upright by Stewart Arnold in a pose similar to the film's phantasmagorical *pas de deux* (all photographed by Bush's brother, John). Album artwork is an important paratext as it 'plays a crucial role in suggesting or confirming the meaning and value of the musical work contained on the record' (Butler 2014: 181). Let us examine that record.

'Rubberband Girl', the opening track, was the album's first single (second in the United States): released on 6 September 1993, it peaked at number 12 in the UK charts, and number 88 in America. A rhythmic 'pure pop' song and one of Bush's most upbeat compositions with a horn section (palely) reminiscent of the Stax sound, it can be read as signalling (not an anticipation of *The Incredibles* (Brad Bird, 2004) but) Bush's determination to return from hardship, 'bouncing back' like the titular elastic. The Confucian notion of bending to circumstances, exhibiting resilience rather than front-on resistance, will be a strong feature of both album and *TLTC&TC*, which 'Rubberband Girl' again opens. Track 2, 'And So Is Love', the album's fifth single which, released on 7 November 1994, reached number 26 in Britain, is a slower bluesy number that relates the end of a love affair (another recurring motif), and how the couple must set each other free. Knowledge that Eric Clapton was honouring a commitment, just two months after the tragic death of his 4-year-old son in New York, could/should add an affecting sense of authenticity to his guitar part: overall, though, his responses to Bush's vocals convey a generic rock sound that jars with the more mythic foundations to Bush's lyrics on ageing and disappointment. This song again features in the film, alongside the next two tracks.

Track 3, 'Eat the Music', the surprising (and non-charting) choice for US lead single, was reviewed as Mexican or Caribbean in feel, but drew inspiration from Madagascan folk music, and its employment of instruments such as the valiha (tube zither) and kabosy (box-shaped guitar) links sonically to *The Red Shoes* film where the ondes Martenot created similarly unexpected textures. Ideologically, the song is related to 'Running Up That Hill': Bush explained to Simon Reynolds how 'It's playing with the idea of opening people up, and the idea of the hidden femininity in a man, and the man in a woman' ('Heaven's Kate', *Melody Maker*, 6 November 1993). Arguably over-ripe in its fruit comparisons ('Split the banana / Crush the sultana!'), Terry Staunton's album review offered a film link to the breakout star of *The Gang's All Here* (Busby Berkeley, 1943) when describing the song as 'a shopping list of exotic fruit, as if Kate is pulling Carmen Miranda's hat apart looking for metaphors for love' (*New Musical Express*, 6 November 1993). For this listener, the exhortation in the chorus to 'split him open / Like a pomegranate' so that 'Insides out / All is revealed', and how 'Not only women bleed' presents a fruit-based counterbalance to *Women in Love* (1969), directed by (Bush-admired) Ken Russell and adapted from D.H. Lawrence's 1920 novel.[2] In particular, it alludes to the scene, interpolated from Lawrence's 1923 poem 'Figs', where school inspector Rupert Birkin (Alan Bates) explains at table (and with relish) how, vulgarly, the fig 'stands for the female part ... the fissure. The yoni. The wonderful moist conductivity towards the centre ... [until] it explodes, and you see through the fissure, the scarlet ... like a wound'. The parallel is rendered explicit on the album's inner artwork (and single's cover-sleeve) which shows soft fruit split open to reveal the red and fleshy vagina-like insides.

Track 4, 'Moments of Pleasure', an accomplished ballad released on 15 November 1993 as the album's third single, became a number 26 UK hit. As noted, this elegiac piece dropped the shield of dramatic personae for a conversational tone that, in its coda, offered a potentially exorcising roll-call of those Bush had recently lost or, with her mother, was losing. Even so, such family memories resonate with film (and album) titles as Bush poignantly sings Hannah's age-consoling aphorism on how 'every old sock meets an old shoe'. Across the song, lyrics that cut between scenes and, like 'The Ninth Wave', enact 'diving off a rock into another moment', possess a cinematic momentum. And while Bush grew increasingly dissatisfied with the song's soundscape (leading her, in the *Director's Cut* re-recording, to remove all instrumentation bar piano and replace the chorus with humming), the final naming of director Powell arguably adds a musical coherence to the original incarnation, notably in its orchestral score. This was arranged and conducted by Michael Kamen (who first worked with Bush on *Brazil*): as Bush recalls the departed, including 'Michael', Kamen's traditional orchestration with lush strings builds and augments the words' weight in the manner of a classic film score. As Hasted argues (though the Archers could replace America): 'Straight Hollywood tearjerking provides a conduit for emotions that the cluttered arrangements elsewhere often obscure' (2022: 92).

Several songs continue Bush's explorations of spiritual and religious realms. Track 5, 'The Song of Solomon', with its imploration to 'Hear a woman singing', chimes with the recalibration of the red shoes story from a female perspective. Named after the sensual love poem aka 'Song of Songs' that constitutes a book of the Old Testament, the song cites lines almost verbatim as it tells of a woman addressing a lover wary of commitment (and/or metaphorically the relationship between God and their followers). Nonetheless, film references again resonate, particularly the invocation to create 'poetry in motion' – in *The Red Shoes* Lady Neston (Irene Browne) defines ballet as 'the poetry of motion'. The promise that 'I'll be Isolde or Marion for you' ties the song to indigenous folklore, but also concurrent screen adaptations. Isolde evokes the chivalric romance with Cornish knight Tristan, recently portrayed in Ireland-set *Fire and Sword* (Veith von Furstenberg, 1981). Marion draws an immediate linkage with Nottingham outlaw Robin Hood and the legend's myriad screen versions, which latterly included Britain's magic-inflected series *Robin of Sherwood* (ITV, 1984–86) and Hollywood's action adventure *Robin Hood: Prince of Thieves* (Kevin Reynolds, 1991). The published spelling – Marion not Marian – offers a further potential allusion, explored next.

Track 6, the esoteric (and *TLTC&TC*-included) 'Lily', is beset with apocalyptic imagery. Even its opening recitation from the Rigveda's Gayatri mantra is backed by 'warbling sound effects' that, for Hasted, 'suggest *Exorcist*-style demons at the door' (2022: 93). This spoken-word introduction is recited by the song's dedicatee, Lily Cornford (1906–2003), a spiritual healer aged 91 on the album's release. Cornford's Maitreya School of Healing practised mental colour therapy, a holistic treatment matching colour energy to client needs – which in the early-1990s included Bush who sings here of not feeling safe and how life has 'blown a great big hole through me'. The song has generated much online debate on the directions of Bush's spiritual leanings (readings include white witchcraft, Isis-worship and Reverse Pentagram Rituals),[3] but pertinent to this study is the appearance of angels. A prominent feature in Hans Christian Andersen's source story (see Chapter 7), Bush told Simon Reynolds that she felt the concept of angels was 'coming forward in the public imagination' – on-screen, alongside the lauded 1986 re-release of *A Matter of Life and Death* one could cite *Always* (Steven Spielberg, 1989), *Graffiti Park* (Prince, 1990) and *Angels* (Philip Saville, ITV, tx. 2 June 1992). Unlike the demons from *The Exorcist* (William Friedkin, 1973), however, these visitors fit more with Cornford's view of angels as 'very powerful, helpful forces' – the opening chant in 'Lily' means to summon celestial assistance for the singer. While the song references the Biblical archangels Gabriel, Raphael, Michael and Uriel (in context 'Michael to my right' can again conjure up director Powell), Bush said she visualised the concept as 'a bit like that film *Wings of Desire* [/ *Der Himmel über Berlin*]', Wim Wenders' 1987 romance where unseen rooftop sentinels observe and empathise with struggling Berliners (Figure 6.1) ('Do Angels Want

Figure 6.1 'Lily' – Angel Eyes.

to Wear Her Red Shoes?', *Pulse*, December 1993). Wenders' film also links back to 'The Song of Solomon' since one of its angels, Damiel (Bruno Ganz), chooses to become mortal after falling in love with a lonely circus trapeze artist – named Marion (Solveig Dommartin).[4]

Track 7, 'The Red Shoes', released on 5 April 1994 as the album's fourth single, reached number 21 in the UK. Alongside its central allusive importance to the LP title and *TLTC&TC* narrative, the song has received discrete academic attention (Gordon 2005), and offers a constructive case study in intent and realisation. Composed at the piano, Bush has explained how, 'Before I had any lyrics, the rhythm of the music led me to the image of horses, something that was running forward, and that led me to the image of the dancing shoes'. Thus she came to Powell and Pressburger's film which (as later discussed) reworks Andersen's fairy tale about a girl possessed by constantly dancing shoes. But whereas the Archers' film retains the source text's notion that dancing can be deadly, Bush's song, free of guest cameos and reeling with its exuberant Irish musical texture, interprets dance as a glorious means to possession, a process that can 'see your eyes are lifted to God' and, by dancing the dream, 'make the dream come true'. Bush explained to Reynolds: 'Musically, I was trying to get a sense of delirium, of something very circular and hypnotic, but building and building ... transcending the normal' (*Melody Maker*, 6 November 1993). Trying, but not fully succeeding? Despite Paddy Bush's rich instrumentation the desired epiphany, that sonic 'lift off', arguably fails to materialise, instead offering evidence in support of Thomson's reserved album judgement. Still, this musical anti-climax will be assessed as aesthetically apposite within the narrative context of *TLTC&TC*.

Track 8, 'Top of the City', again conjures *Wings of Desire* as the singer seeks to be borne 'up on the angels' shoulders' to look down on 'the loneliest city in the world', wherefrom she pines for her lost love. Boasting an achieved musical shift from grounded gospel choir to striped-back rooftop airiness, it nonetheless remains a dislocated number overall, evidenced by the unhelpful additions of Nigel Kennedy (originally laid down in 1990). Clearly significant for Bush, however, along with 'Lily' this was the only album track to feature in her 'Before the Dawn' shows. A musical contrast comes with track 9, 'Constellation of the Heart', Prince-like in its funk flavouring (and name, playing not just on 'Consolations' but Prince's 1985 track 'Condition of the Heart'). It is also the album's most inward-looking number, both for allusions and message. Another track to generate substantial online discussions, (interpretations of its condensed lyrics encompass Freemasonry, Aaron's rod and Michael Moorcock's 1969 sci-fi novel *The Black Corridor*),[5] its self-referentiality is evident as the lyrics repeat lines from 'Moments of Pleasure' ('Just being alive, it can really hurt') and again reference Michael Powell as 'the man with the stick'; like 'Top of the City' they also tell of Heaven and Hell and climbing ladders. However, the focus rests now with telescopes turned inwards and towards the heart: hence 'we point them away from the Big Sky' – a reference back to Bush's 1985 song and its promo video, with the implied significance that now is time to put away childish things, however cherished – such as looking (with Captain Hook telescopes) for shapes in clouds.[6]

'Big Stripey Lie', track 10 (and the B-side to 'Rubberband Girl'), is musically true to its name. Its layered studio construction is throughout 'untrue' to the originally intended live band approach, while Bush taking on the electric guitar part strikes as misguided in what plays like a laboured Captain Beefheart pastiche. Lyrical interpretations have ranged from the Garden of Eden serpent, the Bengal tiger Shere Khan (unctuously voiced by George Sanders in Disney's 1967 animation of Rudyard Kipling's 1894 *The Jungle Book*), or the deceits of romance ('I know I could be good for you'). However glossed, it stays within the album's emotional orbit with references to 'All young dreams drowning / In life's grief'. Track 11, 'Why Should I Love You?', became an interesting amalgam, and not just structurally for its funk-like chorus and wistful verses. Musically the song can sound bloated with Prince overstepping his brief and essentially taking over, all but turning the track Bush sent over to America into a full Paisley Park number with his 48-track contributions on guitar, keyboards, bass, drums and vocals (Jovanovich 2005: 189–190). Bush and Palmer struggled for months (not entirely successfully) to retrieve the song's original feel but, I would argue, it is (re-)tethered to an English sensibility by the (accomplished) last-minute-added backing vocals – the one part not attempted by Prince, though specifically requested by Bush. Knowing that these were provided by Bush's friend, Comic Relief co-founder Lenny Henry, inevitably evokes his raspy baritone soul singer Theophilus P. Wildebeest, a lewd parody based on Teddy Pendergrass and a regular (if divisive) character/caricature on his television series *The Lenny Henry Show* (BBC1, 1984–1988). Henry's homespun harmonies here assist in leavening any residual third-party excesses on the number.[7] Intertextually, asking if a picture exists 'of Jesus laughing', then if he had 'a beautiful smile / A smile that healed' links with the Curve symbol in Bush's film, and repositions the austere and punishing religion portrayed in Andersen's tale with a joyously positive affirmation – indeed, refashions it as a sensual experience if one links the 'Mmm' that divides the song's enquiries to its repeated use in 'The Sensual World'. This concept (though not the song) will be played out in the conclusion to *TLTC&TC*.

The closing track, 'You're the One', another soul-inflected if lumbering number, again addresses an intense love affair's closing. Given the album's strongly autobiographical nature, this has been interpreted (like 'And So Is Love') as treating the end of Bush's relationship with Palmer – significantly(?) Jeff Beck not McIntosh plays lead guitar. Though shorn of overt mythologising, the song (alongside paying homage to guest keyboardist Gary Brooker by citing Procol Harum's 1967 chart-topper 'Whiter Shade of Pale') again calls on film. When Bush declares (twice) that 'I know where I'm going', she augments the album's allusive freight by citing the title of Powell and Pressburger's 1945 metaphysical romance. Again female centred, this film starred Wendy Hiller as Joan Webster, a headstrong Englishwoman who, en route to marry a rich industrialist in the Scottish Hebrides, is marooned by stormy weather on Skye, where she meets and falls in love with Roger Livesey's naval officer (and laird of Kiloran), Torquil MacNeil (Figure 6.2). An explicit example of what the Archers called their 'crusade against materialism' (Macdonald 1994: 242), a term applicable in both philosophical and economic senses, the song's

Figure 6.2 'You're the One' – Looking at The Big Skye.

allusion fits with the spiritual enquiry that plays across *The Red Shoes* album. Also, though the song does not feature in *TLTC&TC*, the evocation of *I Know Where I'm Going!* where Joan finds a guide on her search for self-discovery feeds into the narrative of Bush's film. It also demonstrates conclusively that *The Red Shoes* has not forsaken the music of allusion so fruitfully employed elsewhere in Bush's career.

While similarities in the theme of loss (of life and love) and allusions (to the Archers and others) can loosely tie several songs together, can an overall coherence be found in Bush's *The Red Shoes*? Stephen Dalton, for whom 'any Grand Plan is conspicuously missing', saw only disconnection (*Vox*, November 1993). However, in interview with Roger Trilling, Bush affirmed that the chorus to 'And So Is Love' where she sings of seeing that 'life is sad / And so is love' was not necessarily her belief but a line derived from Joseph Campbell (1904–1987) – who is thanked on the cover credits ('A Tightly Wound Conversation with the Rubberband Girl', *Details*, March 1994).[8] A professor of comparative religion and mythology, Campbell's philosophy has been summarised in his often-repeated mantra, derived from the *Upanishads*, to 'follow your bliss' (Campbell 1988: 120). This quest can be taken as an overarching motivation for *The Red Shoes*, despite its elegiac reflections. A potential patterning in this vein is set out by Jon Young whose album review, unlike Dalton's, seeks to rationalise Bush's 'fevered meditation on the meaning of it all':

Exploring the terrain of the heart in her hyperdramatic way, Bush argues that romance is all we have, even if life stinks ('And So Is Love'), so there's no reason to hold back ('Eat the Music'), that being true to your emotions provides the one sure defense against the darkness ('Lily'), so don't be scared ('Constellation of the Heart'); and follow those desires ('Big Stripey Lie') even if they lead to perdition ('The Red Shoes').

(*Musician*, November 1993)

While a laudable attempt, this patterning will fit less well with *TLTC&TC*. Campbell, though, is also well known for his theory of the archetypal hero, whose journey is shared across world cultures. This 'monomyth' has been hugely influential on film and television, especially since George Lucas credited Campbell's influence on the narrative construction of *Star Wars* (1977) (Kline 1999: 205), and script analyst Christopher Vogler employed his archetypes in developing the standard Hollywood screenwriters' 'bible'/textbook, *The Writer's Journey: Mythic Structure for Storytellers and Screenwriters* (1992). This 'mythic' plot structure will prove particularly pertinent to Bush's film treatment of her album, examined next.

Notes

1. Barratt's nickname came from the teddy bear in children's television show *Andy Pandy* (BBC, 1950–1970) – Bush was rag doll 'Loopy Loo', and sound engineer/producer Jon Kelly was 'Andy' (Thomson 2015: 255).
2. The explicit allusion here also counters Alice Cooper's gender-rigid 'Only Women Bleed', a 1975 Billboard top 20 hit.
3. See, for example, https://katebush.proboards.com/thread/1749 [accessed 14 February 2024].
4. These Wenders-like guardians have endured in Bush's cosmology, reappearing in *50 Words for Snow*'s closing track 'Among Angels'.
5. See, for instance, https://katebush.proboards.com/thread/1750/constellation-heart [accessed 18 February 2024].
6. In a rare late interview with John Wilson, Bush reflected that 'When you lose your mother, you're no longer a little girl any more' (*Front Row*, BBC Radio 4, 4 November 2005).
7. No hard feelings: Bush would provide backing vocals to Prince's 'My Computer' on his 1996 album *Emancipation*.
8. It was also a derivation of its time: re-recorded for her *Director's Cut* album, Bush changed the lyric to 'Now we see that life is sweet'.

7 Strange Phenomena

Kate Bush and *The Line, The Cross & The Curve*

Alongside the approving references to the Archers threaded through *The Red Shoes* album, Kate Bush has explicitly stated her admiration. She underlined to Simon Reynolds how:

> I'm a big fan of Michael Powell's films. They're just very lovely – very sumptuous in their look, but very human as well. There's this lovely sort of heart all the way through his stuff. I also think he had a really wonderful attitude to women, they're always portrayed as women AND as people.

With its distinct title, she made a point of adding that:

> My film is nothing like his film *The Red Shoes* really, but it's based on the same idea of these shoes that have a life of their own, and if you're unfortunate enough to put them on, you're just going to dance and dance.
>
> (*Pulse*, December 1993)

The 'idea' of the dance, and its metonymic embodiment, have a long tradition feeding into Bush's film. This 'back catalogue' is examined first in this chapter, followed by a production and reception history, then full exegesis and evaluation of *TLTC&TC*.

Antecedents

Hilary Davidson, surveying 'the magic of red shoes' and their moulding quality in socio-cultural environments, deems them 'complex and conflicting symbols' (2011: 288). This is certainly the case with the film created by Bush to accompany *The Red Shoes* album, which exemplifies how she takes existing texts and transforms them, especially through a female perspective. *TLTC&TC* follows a three-step process, filtered, alongside her album, through both the original fairy story penned by Hans Christian Andersen, and its film adaptation helmed by Michael Powell. With *The Red Shoes* album already examined, these other antecedents necessitate discrete attention.

Bush had a lifelong interest in child-oriented fairy tales. J.M Barrie's *Peter Pan* narrative, developing from the 1904 Christmas stage play through to its 1953 Disney animation, had featured regularly since Bush's debut album track, 'In Search of Peter Pan'. Later one could offer her *50 Words for Snow* track 'Misty' as not just beefing up Raymond Briggs but reworking Andersen's 'The Snow Man' / 'Sneemanden' (1861), where the eponymous protagonist falls fatally in love with a stove that he feels 'must be of the female sex' (1983: 488).

Andersen's earlier 'The Red Shoes' / 'De Røde Sko' (1845) is, together with the Archers, crucial to *TLTC&TC*. The origin story tells of poor and often barefoot peasant girl Karen who, when given a pair of red cloth shoes by the cobbler's wife, first wears them, proudly but inappropriately, to church at her mother's funeral service. When adopted by a near-blind old lady, Karen tricks her into buying red (rather than the requisite white) leather shoes for her confirmation. Though chastised, she continues to wear them to church, and thinks about them rather than her psalms or prayers. When a mysterious old soldier outside the church labels them dance shoes, they start to dance of their own accord, until put away by her guardian. When the old lady is dying, Karen forgoes her vigil to attend a grand ball and show off her shoes, which again dance of their own volition, forcing Karen, who cannot now remove them, to dance out into the forest. When she reaches the churchyard an angel appears, telling her she will continue to dance until pale and skeleton-thin, a warning to every vain child in the village. She dances for days on end, until she comes to the executioner's house and begs him to cut off her feet: he does so, making her wooden feet and crutches so she can attend church. However, her entry is blocked by the shoes (with her feet inside) dancing before her at the church door. She is taken in by the clergyman's wife as a servant and on Sunday, when she contritely turns to her psalm book, the angel reappears, transforming her room into the church complete with congregation, the organ 'pealing its rich sounds' and 'the children's voices singing in chorus'. Overjoyed at being received back to church, Karen's heart breaks, and 'her soul flies on the sunbeams to heaven' (Andersen 1983: 181–186).

As Jack Zipes notes, Andersen's story 'disseminates notions of childhood that call for the incarceration of the appetites and conformity to the religious penal rules of his times' (2005: 86). This Christian cautionary tale, though, has a distinct gender bias, with pain and punishment meted out to females not just for vanity but for excessively creative (and, to extrapolate, potentially sexual) self-expression. It also indicates the debilitating necessity of being grateful for your subjugation: at the executioner's house, Karen 'kissed the hand that had held the axe' (1983: 184). Bush would appropriate several aspects of the story into both her album and film, such as angelic appearances and the dance towards death. She would, though, challenge its morality, notably the victimisation of the victim, and reclaim the shoes as predominantly a positive, indeed feminist, symbol, uniquely providing their wearer with a narrative voice, and undertaking, as Deborah Withers states, 'to harness them in support of women's creative powers, sustenance and renewal' (2010: 113).

The subsequent transformations of Andersen's story and its potent symbolism have been traced by Davidson back to an initial 'spectacular ballet' version at London's Alhambra Theatre in 1899 (2011: 279). They have continued through to Matthew Bourne's (Archers-inspired) 2016 stage adaptation at Sadler's Wells, and Kim Yong-gyun's 2005 South Korean horror film *The Red Shoes / Bunhongshin*. The most famous version, though, is incontestably Powell and Pressburger's film, which fuses in unparalleled fashion the balletic and cinematic potential of Andersen's tale. A long and complicated gestation, beginning with producer Alexander Korda in 1934 and mixing in the fractious relationship between the Ballets Russes' director Sergei Diaghilev and dancer-choreographer Vaslav Nijinsky, culminated with Pressburger researching Covent Garden rehearsals in 1947, and Scottish ballerina Moira Shearer's casting in the lead role (Macdonald 1994: 275). Along with art directors Hein Heckroth and Arthur Lawson, a ballet score from Brian Easdale, and Jack Cardiff's rich three-strip Technicolor cinematography, this paeon to the art of ballet – and by extrapolation film – broke new ground as 'Powell and Pressburger and their team departed radically from the leitmotif and celebrated genius of British cinema, naturalistic realism' (Connelly 2005: 55).

The resultant film, removed from Andersen's church setting, follows the career of Victoria 'Vicky' Page (Shearer), an aristocratic young dancer who rises to fame with the lead in *The Ballet of The Red Shoes*. Taken on by the Ballet Lermontov, she falls in love with the company's composer Julian Craster (Marius Goring), but its impresario Boris Lermontov (Anton Walbrook), determined nothing shall disrupt his protégée's career, dismisses Julian on hearing of their relationship. Vicky leaves with Julian, but finds married life in London unfulfilling. She agrees to Lermontov's request to 'put on the red shoes again' and revive her signature role, but on opening night Julian delivers an ultimatum – her career or her marriage. She tells Julian that she loves him, but the camera cuts to her red shoes: realising that Vicky still loves dancing,

Julian departs for the railway station. Lermontov raises his arms in triumph but as Vicky heads to the stage her red shoes seemingly impel her to rush after Julian. Leaping from the art nouveau terrace, she is hit by an approaching train. Asking Julian to remove the now-bloodstained shoes, she dies just as the ballet, performed in her honour, ends.

Explaining this violent conclusion, Powell emphasised how *The Red Shoes* negotiates the timeless subject 'that art is worth dying for' (1992: 660). The film presents its female lead with the same dialectic later seen in *Gone to Earth*, where Hazel Woodus is again torn between conflicting patriarchal authorities. Embodied in Julian and Lermontov, here the choice forced on Vicky is in essence between a private life of selfless duty and a public career of artistic self-expression: unable to decide, she chooses death. While not now admonishing nineteenth-century children, *The Red Shoes* remains, like Andersen's text, firmly of its time by enacting the post-war socio-economic pressure on women to resume family-rearing roles and sacrifice their newfound independence/careers. As historian David Kynaston notes, 'the harsh home and/or work dilemma' is 'implacably expounded' in *The Red Shoes* (2008: 209).

Can one determine which side of this dilemma the Archers endorse? While their film never presents Vicky as willingly submissive, her tragic death can be read as supporting the prevailing ideological standpoint that a woman's role lay as homemaker, ostensibly by fitting with a concurrent trend of British cinema – e.g. *Root of All Evil* (Brock Williams, 1947), *This Was a Woman* (Tim Whelan, 1948) – that punished strong women for transgressive ambitions and desires (Aspinall 1983: 284–286). With *The Red Shoes*, though, this hegemonic ending can equally be seen as failing to cohere with the body of a film that consistently relishes female daring and personal fulfilment, and that so purposefully pushes us 'to sympathise with the pleasure of Vicky's artistic aspirations and the unfairness of her social position' (Sheil 2008: 68).

Replicating this ambivalence, the centrepiece of *The Red Shoes* – and principal influence on Bush – was its 'film within a film', the 17-minute phantasmagorical sequence portraying the premiere of the work that made Vicky Page famous. Narratively closer to Andersen, *The Ballet of The Red Shoes* shows the Girl (Shearer) being tempted by a pair of red shoes on display in the window of the church-adjacent Shoemaker's shop. The Shoemaker (former Ballets Russes maestro Léonide Massine) encourages her desire while her boyfriend entreats her to resist. In vain: once the shoes are on her feet, the Boy withdraws and the Girl, unable to stop dancing or return home from a carnival to her aged guardian, undertakes a frenetic passage through a series of dark dreamscapes (Figure 7.1), where characters from Vicky's 'real life' appear on stage. Lermontov suddenly stands

Figure 7.1 The Red Shoes – Total Film.

before her, as does Julian, anticipating Vicky's life/art dilemma. Danseur Ivan Boleslawsky (Robert Helpmann, also sequence choreographer), having played the Boy, reappears as a print-wrapped embodiment of the Press, then a Prince for the euphoric *pas de deux*. Led by the demonic Shoemaker, the Girl/Vicky's psychic journey takes in a grand ball, an animalistic red-light district and, again anticipating Vicky's fate, a 'City of the Dead' where monstrous skeletal figures surround and bear her aloft. Finally the Girl returns from this surreal geography to the town square: as upright citizens enter church for her guardian's funeral service, she begs the local parson (Boleslawsky again) for salvation. When he unties the shoes, the Girl collapses into his arms: the smiling Shoemaker, who gave her a knife, picks up the shoes and offers them to the audience. Curtain.

There is a danger in departing radically from indigenous cinematic traditions and paying mere lip-service to expected ideological resolutions, and Britain's reception for *The Red Shoes* was decidedly mixed: the *mise en abyme* of the ballet sequence, merging realist and fantasy discourses, bemused as much as bewitched the critics. The trade press, for instance, found that Powell and Pressburger 'have fumbled over a fine idea, and their opulent work trembles between the heights and the depths' (*Daily Film Renter*, 22 July 1948). In America the film was more positively received, moving quickly from art house to mainstream circuits: Bosley Crowther typically lauded how 'there has never been a picture in which the ballet and its special, magic world have been so beautifully and dreamily presented' and deemed it 'a film you must see' (*New York Times*, 23 October 1948).[1] Assisted by such endorsements, *The Red Shoes* became the first British film to gross $5 million-plus at the US box-office, received five Academy Award nominations, and won for Art Direction and Original Score. It has subsequently enjoyed a wide address, among both connoisseurs and the general public. It was placed ninth in the BFI's 1999 poll of critics and filmmakers to find 'the greatest British films of the twentieth century', and number 67 in its 2022 poll for the 'greatest films of all time'. It is also widely acknowledged for inculcating an interest in dance/ballet to generations of young people – an influence referenced in the backstage musical *A Chorus Line* (Richard Attenborough, 1985) when dancer Diana Morales (Yamil Borges) claims, in her audition, to have seen the film 112 times. Bush too would show the influence of *The Red Shoes*, bringing to fruition a long-held ambition to advance her artistic deployment of the moving image.

Production and Reception

Cooling on the notion of touring *The Red Shoes*, Bush determined instead, late in recording, to create a longer film, largely based on Powell and Pressburger's reworking of Andersen, as a companion piece and alternative promotional tool for her album. There were precedents for such an undertaking. *The Red Shoes*' fantasy ballet had formally inspired several films, notably the extended dance sequences in *An American in Paris* (Vincente Minnelli, 1951) and *Singin' in the Rain* (Stanley Donen, Gene Kelly, 1952).[2] Closer to home, Bush may have been influenced by the example of her LP collaborators. Prince's semi-autobiographical film debut *Purple Rain* (Albert Magnoli, 1984) had facilitated his rise to superstar status, winning the Academy Award for Best Original Song Score and globally shifting 25 million soundtrack album copies. Bush may also have recalled being one of the happy few to see Jeff Beck's cameo appearance at David Bowie's final Ziggy Stardust concert: Pennebaker's film of the Hammersmith Odeon event (minus Beck but with soundtrack album) enjoyed an international release in 1983.[3] Even Lenny Henry had successfully hit the big screen with his Hackney Empire-recorded *Lenny Live and Unleashed* (Andy Harries, 1989), the first British stand-up show to gain a cinema release.

The lateness of her decision, however, meant that Bush was rushed to realise her debut film project. Once green-lit by EMI (and funded for $1 million), her 50-minute piece was written and rehearsed in two months, then filmed over three weeks at London's Black Island Studios (plus location work at Aldwych Underground Station). It was an ambitious venture, especially since, as with her recent video releases, Bush not only handled scriptwriting and choreography, but also assumed the role of actor-director, and involved herself heavily in post-production.

She followed past practice, though, in establishing a skilled and trusted support network. For her *Ballet of the Red Shoes* variant, Bush brought in two co-stars that had bookended her career to date, early dance instructor Lindsay Kemp, and recent *Comic Strip* colleague Miranda Richardson, now a potential international entrée after big screen successes with *The Crying Game* (Neil Jordan, 1992) and *Damage* (Louis Malle, 1992), the latter earning her a Best Supporting Actress Academy Award nomination. Behind the camera, Margarita Doyle was chosen as producer, a role she had effected on Bush's 'Rocket Man' video after a long association with Terry Gilliam (himself credited for specialist camera provision). Julian Doyle returned as technical advisor; Roger Pratt, later to work on *Lake Tahoe*, handled cinematography; experienced production designer Roger Hall became Art Director alongside Ben Scott; former *Monty Python* alumni Bob Hollow and Hazel Pethig came in as special effects director and costume designer respectively. All helped to create the production's desired phantasmagorical look, while Julian Rodd, whose career began on Roeg's *Castaway*, assisted Bush with the (difficult) editing process.

TLTC&TC featured six album tracks: 'Rubberband Girl', 'And So Is Love', 'The Red Shoes' (twice reprised), 'Lily', 'Moments of Pleasure', and 'Eat the Music'. Despite its holistic artistic intentions, all bar 'Lily' would be discretely extracted as promo videos for the relevant singles – even a new US video for 'Rubberband Girl' featured clips from Bush's film. This synergistic strategy undoubtedly explains *TLTC&TC*'s television-friendly 1.33 aspect ratio.

Although Bush was allowed to delay her album release to synchronise with the film's completion, she still felt considerable pressure during a fraught shoot, later admitting that 'I felt like I hadn't put enough time into it … It hadn't been thought through properly' (Doyle 2022: 243). While primarily marketed at the Video Home System (VHS) market, Bush met her target to premiere the film, complete with Dolby digital sound, at the 37th London Film Festival on 13 November 1993, an event Bush attended with her father and (keeping up appearances) with Del Palmer. In tandem with the release of 'The Red Shoes' single, *TLTC&TC*

was exhibited as a support feature at selected UCI cinemas across Britain from 6 May 1994. Limited US theatre showings followed.

The official press release, penned by Bush, offers the following plot summary (and character descriptors) for the film:

> One evening, two dancers (Kate Bush, Stewart Arnold) are rehearsing for a show in a hot, humid room during a brewing storm. When lightning strikes and cuts the power, Kate is left alone in the darkened room in an introspective mood. Suddenly out of the mirror bursts a woman (Miranda Richardson) in a mysterious dress. Her hands are bandaged and on her feet she wears a pair of beautiful red shoes. She is deeply distressed or so she wishes us to believe and as she tells a tale of lies she tricks Kate into drawing three symbols – a line, a cross and a curve. Kate innocently obliges by handing over her 'soul' and acquiring the red shoes that are possessed by dance. In triumph the successful trickster leaps back into her own world and the red shoes carry Kate through the doorway in the mirror. A guide comes to her side (Lindsay Kemp) and he explains how the only way to break the spell is to sing back the symbols. And so begins a journey of possession and madness – a dance to hell and back on the other side of the mirror.

Bush's character (offering an avowedly personal link in being named Kate) undertakes three trials, successfully wrestles back the shoes from the Woman, and returns through the mirror to the real world.

At its London premiere, *TLTC&TC* formed an unlikely double-bill with Aardman Animation's *The Wrong Trousers* (Nick Park, 1993). Both works were rapturously applauded on the night, but their subsequent receptions could scarcely be more different. While *The Wrong Trousers* won 1994's Academy Award for Best Animated Short, unanimous eulogies, and has become a staple of holiday television scheduling, Bush's effort largely slipped through the critical cracks and its few contemporaneous reviews, while not dire, were underwhelming.[4] UK-based David Elley wrote that 'Shyly retiring pop diva Kate Bush, 35, steps behind the lens with mixed artistic results in *The Line, The Cross & The Curve*, a music promo flick high on whimsy and low on content' but 'a solid bet for special events, with eight numbers sure to please Bush aficionados'. He found that, 'When not warbling, Bush is colourless' while 'Pic's visual style is relatively conservative, far from the usual musicvid fare' (*Variety*, 6 December 1993). America's Chris Willman was more onside:

Obviously Bush isn't about to improve upon the classic 1948 Michael Powell film that was her inspiration ... But Powell might approve of her filmmaking's richly lit, darkly colorful leitmotifs. And Bush is less interested in homage than using the shoe shtick as launch pad for a series of independent, increasingly surreal music-vid vignettes.

He concluded that 'she gets to shimmy with aplomb, of course not Shearer, but not bad' and termed her 'an agreeably earthy etherealist' (*Los Angeles Times*, 1 July 1994).

As Willman's review shows, *TLTC&TC*, like *The Red Shoes* film, was better received on its (belated) US promotion, and earned a 1996 Grammy nomination for Best Music Video, Long Form. Released on VHS (and laserdisc in Japan) in late-1994, it has not (as of March 2024) received a DVD or streaming release, though it continues to appear sporadically at arthouse cinemas and festivals.[5] Bush herself was less than bullish in promotional interviews. She emphasised that the experience had been 'really interesting for me, really educational', but bemoaned the short rehearsal and filming period – 'we should really have had twice as long' – and questioned its exhibition potential – 'I've no idea where it will actually be shown, but it would be nice for people to get to see it in its entirely. Just once!' (*Pulse*, December 1993). Looking back, she would (infamously) lambast her acting, especially next to Richardson's, as 'a load of old bollocks' (Doyle 2005: 81): it is an appraisal often, but erroneously, attributed to the whole project. Nonetheless, her surrounding discourse indicates immediate and enduring reservations, and the film was quietly dropped. Add in the subsequent decade-long hiatus in Bush's career, and *TLTC&TC* sank into obscurity.

Over the next three decades its reputation scarcely improved, especially in Bush biographies. For Jovanovich, 'The acting is OK and the dancing is good in patches, but as a complete experience it is quite poor – certainly one of the most disappointing things she's produced' (2005: 194). Thomson is particularly vitriolic, assessing that:

> for someone with her cinematic knowledge, her love of the form, her talent and desire for perfectionism, to achieve little more than the typically overblown Eighties and Nineties 'concept' video – inflated, badly acted, rambling, wracked with faux-profundity, everything coated with that shallow glossy sheen – was a bitter disappointment.
>
> (2015: 279)

However, the tide (especially in the wake of *Stranger Things*) is, perhaps, turning. *TLTC&TC* featured in the 'Lost and Found' section of September 2022's august *Sight and Sound* magazine where Alex Ramon declared that it 'rewards reappraisal with its bold visuals and witty cinematic references'. Though finding Bush's performance 'flat', he was more forgiving than Bush herself, noting that 'her movement and vocalising are expressive, and visually she recalls screen icons from Lillian Gish to Liz Taylor'. He emphasised how she is particularly 'powerful in the musical interludes' (2022: 99). The following exegesis looks to further that reappraisal, remaining fully vigilant to the work's failings alongside its felicities.

Analysis

Concomitant to providing a compendium of Bush's video themes and tropes to date (and, in places, to come), *TLTC&TC* is steeped in cinematic allusion. First, Bush's film fits into a broad genealogy of female directors eschewing classic realism for poetic and avant-garde productions. She follows in the dance/footsteps of French surrealist Germaine Dulac, famed for the sensual hallucinations (and critique of patriarchy) in *The Seashell and the Clergyman / La Coquille et Le Clergyman* (1928); plus Ukrainian-born American Maya Deren, also a dancer-choreographer, best known for her radically experimental (and symbol-filled) *Meshes of the Afternoon* (1943). Alongside the rampant intertextuality of *TLTC&TC*, its loosely plotted quest narrative, female leads, and engaging dance numbers – plus directorial disappointment at the result – resonate particularly with London-born Sally Potter's feminist experimental debut, *The Gold Diggers* (1983).[6]

More specifically, *TLTC&TC* is augmented by the presentation of a near-taxonomy of footwear in film. Kate playing happily with her new shoes explicitly references Charlie Chaplin's Dance of the Oceana Roll in *The Gold Rush* (Chaplin, 1925), a poignant and intimate fantasy sequence where, on New Year's Eve, Chaplin's broke and lovelorn Lone Prospector entertains (absent) guests by representing a ballet dancer's feet with two fork-speared bread rolls manipulated beneath his chin (Figure 7.2). As Eric Reinholtz notes, with his redeployment of food 'the tramp must subvert social codes and undermine the mundane in order to obtain those things the world denies him' (2012: 268). It is a transgressive action in an otherworldly space that Kate will similarly undertake.

108 *Film*

Figure 7.2 The Line, The Cross & The Curve – Bush Meets Chaplin.

Red shoes, and real-life characters invading fantasy sequences, chime with the adventures of Dorothy Gale (Judy Garland) in *The Wizard of Oz* (Victor Fleming, 1939), adapted from Frank L. Baum's 1900 children's novel. *TLTC&TC*, like Fleming's film, can be categorised as a portal/quest fantasy where, as Farah Mendelsohn precises, 'a character leaves her familiar surroundings and passes into an unknown space' (2008: 1). The positive ending to *TLTC&TC*, with Kate finding enlightenment and 'coming home', parallels Dorothy and Oz rather than *The Red Shoes* film, as does channelling the shoes' power into a positive force, protecting her against her witching nemesis. Specifically, the Woman's final sighting in *TLTC&TC*, buried under rubble with only her (reshod) feet visible, replays Dorothy's house landing on the Wicked Witch of the East, previous wearer of the ruby slippers. Withers detects a further allusion with Bush's three symbols comparable to the brain, heart and courage, respectively sought by Dorothy's Scarecrow, Tin Man and Lion companions (2010: 113).

Another prime example, alluded to in Bush's choice of portal, is [*Alice*] *Through the Looking-Glass*, Lewis Carroll's 1871 novel most famously filmed (combined with Carroll's 1865 prequel) in Disney's 1951 *Alice in Wonderland*, but discretely and more darkly adapted for

UK television by director James MacTaggart (BBC1, tx. 25 December 1973). Peter Bradshaw would later recognise the horror contained in Powell and Pressburger's *Ballet of the Red Shoes*, comparing it to 'the surface of Lewis Carroll's looking-glass, through which the viewer is transported into a new world of amazement and occult horror' (*Guardian*, 10 December 2009). Bush sensed this too and foregrounds the parallel in *TLTC&TC*.

The mirror passage to a dangerous world, plus the appearance of guardian angels, also echo Jean Cocteau's first feature, *The Blood of a Poet / Le Sang d'un Poète* (1930), another symbol-filled exploration of the pleasures and especially pains of being an artist. Behind such adventures one can trace the narrative patterning summarised by mythologist Joseph Campbell:

> A hero ventures forth from the world of common day into a region of supernatural wonder: fabulous forces are there encountered and a decisive victory is won: the hero comes back from this mysterious adventure with the power to bestow boons on his fellow man.
>
> (1968: 23)

The gender may be over-determined, but the (optional) 17 stages Campbell adumbrated include (at three) supernatural aid / meeting with a mentor, (seven) meeting with the goddess, (10) apotheosis, and (17) freedom to live, stages onto which can be mapped the meetings of Kate with Kemp and Cornford her transformation during 'Eat the Music', and her concluding liberation to resume artistic production.

Traceable also in *TLTC&TC* is the personalising influence of previously employed reference points. *Night of the Demon*, adapted from M.R. James' 1911 story 'Casting the Runes', is again present in the borrowed plot line where symbol-bearing slips of paper confer great power – their supernatural passing to the Woman with the sound of wind, and her desperate chase for them through darkness come straight from Tourneur's film. Kemp's mysterious Guide, reflected in mirrors and lurking in shadows, recalls Clayton's *The Innocents* and the haunting presence of valet Peter Quint. The Guide's pained clutching of red-dressed lifeless Kate and the subsequent search for psychic intervention reflect the iconography and narrative development of *Don't Look Now*. The Guide's presence on Kate's spiritual quest, alongside fitting Campbell's patterning, parallels the character dynamic (minus the romance) from Powell and Pressburger's *I Know Where I'm Going!* where Joan's self-discovery is aided by Torquil, and especially their previous *A Canterbury Tale* where, with its (Bush-like) mix of

Paganism and Christianity, land girl Alison Smith (Sheila Sim)'s 'pilgrimage' to Canterbury is prompted by the older enigmatic 'glue-man' aka magistrate Thomas Colpeper (Eric Portman).

The red thread through Bush's film is, of course, *The Red Shoes*. This was an attempt to create what Powell called 'composed' or 'total film', a concept explained by Raymond Durgnat when terming its ballet sequence 'a montage of shots ... but also of different art forms', resulting in 'an art of all the arts, a *gesamtkunstwerk*, a non-realistic spectacle' (Schoonmaker et al. 2003: 156). This was Bush's aim also, to extend and enmesh her extant recording practice, packaging strategies, stage performances and video activity by seeking, as she had evidenced with David Bowie, 'a multisensory synthesis of art forms' (Perrott 2024:5). Differently, though, she would work, at narrative, visual and auditory levels, to ensure a greater self-determined female agency. A close chronological analysis will evaluate how successfully Bush fares in these aims.

As Andrew Moor notes, *The Red Shoes* film 'is marked by ambiguities: art is supernatural, inspired, demonic, but it is also the product of graft and skill' (2005: 198). It is (like *A Chorus Line*) a process film that surrounds its 'magical' performance set-piece with 'authentic' sets and rehearsal scenes – even *The Ballet of the Red Shoes* begins on a realistic stage before entering Vicky's expressionist nightmare. *TLTC&TC* also opens in rehearsal mode, complementing the source film's dual focus on the verisimilitude of backstage preparation and the melodrama of its fantastical staged dances. While Bush's music and videos are normally a celebration of achieved rhythm and imaginative movement, 'Rubberband Girl' (4.33 minutes) shows the artist struggling to create to desired levels. Matching the self-doubt of the song's opening lyrics, this beginning sets the premise for the film and intimates how far the committed artist must/will go to find correct self-expression.

This visualisation thus allows a further, literal interpretation to the song and its central metaphor. The camera follows trombonist Neil Sidwell into the dance studio, its cramped and dingy conditions distinctly non-magical, then loops 360 degrees, indicating a locale lacking physical and mental equilibrium. Kate, casually dressed and barefoot (like Karen), sings and works on a set of dance moves with Arnold, reminiscent of Shearer and Helpmann, but more closely evoking the entwined choreography to 'Hammer Horror' and 'Running Up That Hill', (plus a late tango recalling 'Hounds of Love'). Here, though, the moves are unsatisfactory – Kate aborts their practice after the first chorus, then resumes with several clumsy movements, first on the studio floor, briefly atop the piano, even solo jumping (with exasperation rather than release) high into the air. Her dissatisfaction and distanciation are evident (and later voiced after another abandoned practice): she wants to be more subtle, rubberband-like as a dancer – not the restricted version indicated by needing a rubberband to 'hold me trousers up' and make ponytails.

So she pushes further. Bush's efforts over her career have drawn epithets to the effect that she is 'eccentric', 'anormative', even a 'crazy lady', and three minutes in Arnold wraps her in a straitjacket – a move readable as wry self-deprecating humour and/or proudly taking ownership of such epithets (Figure 7.3).[7] A prop also used in 'Experiment IV', the straitjacket intimates the relationship/overlap, repeatedly adumbrated in her work, between musical innovation and perceived 'madness'. In the context of the mythic/narrative structures she is now reworking, it also indicates the restraints that the inherent patriarchal values of the red shoes story (and other backstage works) present to the female artist. Even here Kate is tightly surrounded by eight male musicians, and twice Danny McIntosh steps forward to foreground the song's virtuoso 'cock rock' guitar solos.

Figure 7.3 The Line, The Cross & The Curve – 'We Let the Weirdness In'.

As 'Rubberband Girl' finishes, a giant electric fan breaks into the studio, followed by its hapless operator (*Comic Strip* colleague Peter Richardson). This manages to clear the air (in all senses): as well as bringing a comic sensibility to the piece – an early (and arguably underused) modulation of tone – it curtails the rehearsal and, coupled with a power cut closing operations 'for at least half-an-hour', sends all bar Kate away, freeing the space for the melancholic 'And So Is Love' (5.32 minutes). Now wearing a long black dress with (rubberband-held) hair up, she lights a candle (for her torch song) while lightning flashes overhead. Musical scores are scattered about the room, blown there by the errant fan but again suggestive of creative struggle. A quiet passage amidst the storm, with plentiful soft-focus close-ups on the singer, Bush's performance can be seen as self-referential: she has already made the Vicky Page choice, sacrificing love for art – but an art as yet unattainable.

When, late in the song, a blackbird enters the studio, hits a window and falls dead on her music score, Kate kisses the body and lays it on red velvet. The poet Wallace Stevens drew up 'Thirteen Ways of Looking at a Blackbird' and, with symbolic intent evident, the dying bird offers several readings, beginning as a (clunking) signifier of the relationship described in the song. Narratively, it relates to the entrapped nature of the dancer's heart and desires (as further sheet music later testifies), and presages entries to come. Blackbirds also featured in Bush's earlier mythology, notably 'Waking the Witch' ('Help this blackbird! / Wake the witch'): with the dark stormy cadre evoking the horror genre, it potentially prompts the perception of Kate having a 'previous familiarity with magick' (Withers 2010: 122).

Richardson's mysterious monobrowed Woman straightaway breaks through from the mirror world (drawn by sensing Kate's supernatural potential?). Her exaggerated 'Oirish' accent as she relates her dilemma recalls the dangers of engagement played out in Bush's 'Army Dreamers'; it equally resonates with Richardson's BAFTA-nominated role in *The Crying Game* as Jude, the deceptive IRA member who sets a honey trap for British soldier Jody (Forest Whitaker). Kate – whose initial responses of 'Jesus!' and 'What the hell is going on?' offer both indications of a spiritual quest and an artistic hostage to fortune – is duped by the Woman's pleas, but also seems unphased by the entreaty to draw the eponymous spell-breaking symbols on paper strips. This scene shows Bush moving away from the Andersen and Archers versions to create a fresh (eponymous) symbolic logic for a female-centred mythology, explained (with increasing menace, it should be noted) by the Woman and reiterated in the song: 'And this curve, is your smile / And this cross, is your heart / And this line, is your path'.

While primarily informed by Michael Powell, Bush's other 'tremendous influence', Alfred Hitchcock, is traceable in brief allusions. The Woman's hands, bandaged, she says, because of 'a big fire', link with Hitchcock's spy thriller *Saboteur* (1942) which, following the suspected arson attack on a California aircraft factory, opens with an eye-witness report from security guard Rogers (Will Lee), his burnt hands similarly covered in thick bandages as he describes how, with flames catching, 'it was just like all hell comes up'. Regarding narrative motivation, one can read this visitor as the woman Kate wants to be – not just nimble on her feet ('Oh she move like the Diva do') but exotically dressed and, as the bandages show, living dangerously. She prompts a duplication of the transition Bush's 'librarian' undertakes in the Hitchcockian 'Hounds of Love' video, as again her hair 'come[s] tumbling down', freed of its restrictive rubberband.

Presented as a gift of gratitude, Kate is tricked into accepting the Woman's footwear – satin ballet shoes coloured red, or more precisely, as in the Archers' film, crimson lake aka carmine. The transaction leads into the pair performing 'The Red Shoes' (4.02 minutes). Though not titular, it constitutes the film's primary (and reprised) track, and its first employment remained, for Bush, 'the one thing I think works really well in the film' (Doyle: 2022: 244).[8] Bonnie Gordon notes how the 'plurality of voices, the endless repetition of the song that defies closure, and the sometimes dissonant meanings resist a fixed interpretation' (2005: 43). Enacting that vocal plurality, the performance of Bush and Richardson together begins benignly, toying with the shoes like Chaplin, and offers an effective (and amusing) retort to previous video boycotts in Bush's career (cf. 'Running Up That Hill' and 'Cloudbusting') by having the song lip-synched – but *not* by Kate/Bush, switching instead to the newly liberated Woman/Richardson, who promises the frustrated artist than now it will be 'the way you always dreamt about it'. Here we witness the film's first doubling, as the protagonists swap voices and meld in the choreography (more successfully than earlier with Arnold). On donning the footwear Kate realises she has 'done something wrong' and the bandages unfurl from the Woman's hands precisely as the shoes' ribbons tie themselves onto Kate's feet – the latter an exact replay of the special effects close-up of Vicky Page on stage. When the

Woman escapes back though the studio's mirrored walls, the shoes' new wearer is constrained to follow her into a testing 'City of the Dead', its floor skull-covered and aflame.[9]

It is at this transitional point that Lindsay Kemp's otherworldly Guide enters, effecting the triangular character dynamic also played out in *The Red Shoes*. However, there is no polycule of tension and/or resentment as Kemp's presence, obviating heteroromantic connotations, supports a narrative where Kate (re-)finding her identity is not dependent on 'finding a man'. He also functions in an opposite direction to the Woman and 'The Red Shoes' song: he first seemingly embodies malevolence, enticing Kate towards danger with a white-painted face reminiscent of Massine's demonic Shoemaker, but the make-up equally references Kemp's best-known life-affirming mime performances, and here, informing Kate that she must 'sing back the symbols' to break the curse, he reveals himself as helpful and trustworthy – and apposite casting given Kemp's importance in Bush's own early career.

The Guide, a regular character in portal/quest fantasies, is here a complex (or confusing?) character. His later calming of Kate's dancing shoes by splaying out his hands suggests an incantatory power similar, but again opposed in employment, to the Shoemaker, and to Andersen's old soldier. Indicative of *TLTC&TC*'s pervasive doublings/divisions, he (sporadically) sports a cane which, alongside impresarios such as Diaghilev, recalls the sung reference to Michael Powell in 'Moments of Pleasure'. This connection is reinforced with a knowledge of *The Red Shoes* film's inspirations. As Moor notes, 'The Ballet Lermontov is held up as a mirror for the Archers' own company' and Lermontov's 'tyrannical power' in pursuit of artistic perfection is consistently read as a thinly veiled and self-aware portrayal of Powell himself (2005: 204).

Though beckoned by the Guide, Kate's portal passage initially fails: she is neither trained nor dressed for the *en pointe* advance first attempted. Indicative of moves (and messages) to come, it is by running naturally and resolutely that she passes through. Now clearly assuming the Woman's place in sporting the same black-and-red dress, this section most fully condenses *The Ballet of the Red Shoes*. Pamela Hutchinson notes that 'Vicky must dance with her demons to achieve greatness' (2023: 95): Bush's take, despite the charnel-house mise-en-scène, is a sumptuous four minutes, largely joyous and non-too serious – two camp, red-suited devils even appear (Paddy Bush and Colin Lloyd Tucker) to join in the merriment, standing to dance (like the dervishes in her 'Love and Anger' video) just as Kate/Bush sings to 'call a priest'. And though the red shoes myth propounds a loss of control, she sings that 'I'm gonna dance the dream' and 'make the dream come true' as a path *willingly* taken to fulfil her terpsichorean aspirations.

The new pairing of Kate and her Guide are shown enjoying their dancing. Jigging as to an Irish reel, jiving as to rock'n'roll, there is, significantly, no rigidity of trained, constrained movement: as Withers notes, Kate's 'possession by the shoes does not mean she has no power to dismember the ballet form' (2010: 116–117). Indeed, contextualising *TLTC&TC* within Bush's career to date, this section registers not as progressing to new levels of cultural 'sophistication', but rather a return to Bush's earlier, 'innocent' and less worked-through video practice – a desire also sought at the outset of recording *The Red Shoes* album. Thus Kemp's casting again signifies: her mentor for the early MacMillan-directed dance videos, Bush even wrote a song in Kemp's honour, 'Moving', that opened *The Kick Inside*. There she noted his instruction on movement: 'Don't think it over, it always takes you over / And sets your spirit dancing'. Here Bush returns to such basics, ignoring concomitant criticisms of 'am dram' performances. Thus, smiling with abandon amidst her travails, one can add a biographical layer to Gordon's claim that the red shoes story is here most fully transformed into 'precisely what it is meant to denigrate – the dance of female excess' (2005: 45).

As the pair dance, Hitchcock's influence resurfaces. The stylised depiction of demonic fire with multi-coloured streamers blowing vertically behind them registers (like 'Running Up That Hill') with Hitchcock's *Torn Curtain*, in particular its climactic ballet scene where an identical on-stage recreation of flame-filled cauldrons prompts an alarmist call of 'Fire!', allowing its leads to escape their East Berlin pursuers. Here there is no escape (yet) as the shoes' power takes over and the lyrical refrain of 'You gotta dance!' takes on a late fresh/frightening resonance, stridently recalibrating Gene Kelly's *Singin' in the Rain* admission as Bush's feet flutter unnaturally quickly (though still potentially comically) above the skull-laden floor. The song's inability to 'transcend the normal' as Bush intended (see Chapter 6) here becomes narratively apposite, as Kate collapses exhausted into the Guide's arms – (alongside *Don't Look Now*) another direct parallel to the ballet sequence's closure in Powell and Pressburger, though it arguably initiates an overused/facile section ending in *TLTC&TC* where Bush repeatedly gestures to states beyond or below conscious control (Figure 7.4).

While the Woman runs off down a long tunnel triumphantly waving the three symbols, the Guide calms a troubled Kate, whose call for a knife again matches the source film. Her posture, though, seated while

Figure 7.4 The Line, The Cross & The Curve – Death and the Maiden.

her legs (clearly a second body) thrash about in ungainly fashion, (comically) parodies the overtly sensual choreography of Bush's video for 'The Man with the Child in His Eyes'. The Guide's role, however, is not that of saviour and instead he directs Kate towards a female-centred support network. This initially continues *TLTC&TC*'s biographical layer, as Kemp hands over to Bush's most recent real-life mentor – 'let's go see Lily', he instructs.

'Lily' (4.05 minutes), a narrative turning-point (though indifferently realised), features nonagenarian colour-therapist Lily Cornford herself, appearing in a flash of special effects on a white wicker-backed chair and reiterating that Kate must 'sing back the symbols'. While again aiming to share the song's vocals, Cornford's lip-synching is derisory, swiftly breaking a different spell, that of viewer engagement. More propitiously, she wears a calming pale-blue shirt and, suggestive of role-doubling with the Guide, has a cane hanging from her chair. For Doyle she effects 'a serenely otherworldly, almost David Lynchian film character' (2022: 244): a (more) skilled exponent of magic, she offers Kate hope through a ritual practice where she creates a 'circle of fire' with her cane and summons the archangels Gabriel, Raphael, Michael and Uriel (Christopher Banaman, John Chesworth, Vernon Nurse and Robert Smith) for protection.

Intertextually, Lily's Gayatri invocation to reveal the face of the Spiritual Sun, 'Hidden by a disc of golden Light', recalls the (cardboard cut-out) visual imagery employed in Bush's videos for 'Delius (Song of Summer)' and, especially given its fulcrum function, the two-part 'Breathing'. Holding each other tightly and slowly revolving as Kate relates her fears of walking 'in the Vale of Darkness' appositely echoes the minimalist choreography of Bush's duet with Peter Gabriel on 'Don't Give Up'. Ideologically, however esoteric the ritual – Withers informs it 'will be recognised by practitioners of classic Kabbalah as the Lesser Banishing Ritual of the Pentagram' (2010: 123) – the visualisation of the four white-robed angels indicates a shift in mythic sourcing from Andersen, pointedly asserting that (Christian) religious power here functions as protection and guidance, not a tool for female pain and punishment. Their solemn surrounding of Kate as her journey resumes may be weakened by unmotivated jump-cut editing, but we are firmly in the domain of Wenders' movie rather than Victorian morality.

As 'Lily' concludes, the sword-wielding archangel Michael (Powell?) draws a line in the snow, indicating – as the Guide's voiceover clarifies - that 'the spell is being broken' and Kate has sung back her path symbol. Despite this positive development, a howling wind and reprise of the instrumental opening to 'The Red Shoes' now accompany Kate as she undergoes her next ordeal. The scene again alludes to *The Red Shoes* as Kate places her hands either side of her face, reproducing the iconic close-up of Vicky taking fright on stage and occasioning the dream ballet sequence. Here, though, a letterbox emphasis on Kate's eyes also recalls 'Army Dreamers' and 'The Big Sky', while the image turning in full circles offers intratextual stylistic links both to *TLTC&TC*'s beginning and the subsequent section where Kate floats through star-filled space. An effective internalisation for Kate/Bush telling rather than showing, she narrates in voice-over (initially echoing Samuel Beckett's 1953 novel *The Unnamable*) how 'I can't go on. I'm torn between what I was and what is to become of me', and undertakes a sustained and self-reflective monologue. Recognising how 'In these shoes every step I take is laced with madness', her disclosure that 'I see streets and buildings I know so well, although I have never been to these places' highlights the vicarious/depersonalising nature of Bush's allusive modus operandi. Noting how 'we tripped from a stage into the pit. I see me falling' adds the theatrical and vertiginous elements emphasised in the Archers' film. Recalling how 'we raced with wild horses till they dropped' references the equine imagery that initiated Bush's composition of 'The Red Shoes' and thereafter the entire album-film concept.

118 *Film*

At this point of low morale (if heightened meta-textuality), the Guide again intervenes. His imploration for Kate to 'call upon those you love' leads into 'Moments of Pleasure' (4.32 minutes) and its allusion-light sharing of bereavement. The number's film representation (though retrospectively anticipating 'And Dream of Sheep (Live)') similarly eschews visual complexity and overt intertextuality. Continuing the monologue's background dislocation of forms but now alternating realism (an abandoned orchestra pit) and artifice (an abstraction of New York skyscrapers) in loose accord with the lyrics' progression, Kate/Bush sings directly to camera while slowly twirling, arms aloft, through this spiritually liminal space.[10] The hint of a smile appears as the joy of movement gives her the strength to continue her battle, her spoken 'I can't go on' visually countered with 'I'll go on' (Figure 7.5).

The red shoes, deemed inappropriate when worn by Andersen's Karen on her mother's death, are here decisively revised. When Kate/Bush recalls those departed (now including her mother), snow falls heavily and representations of the characters named are slowly blown past her in the storm. Not straining for impersonation, the actors employed bear scant resemblance to the lost ones – with Michael Powell, for instance, a pony-tailed young man drifts past. This casting strategy renders what critics found an 'impenetrable' and 'solipsistic'

Figure 7.5 The Line, The Cross & The Curve – 'I Can't Go On: I'll Go On'.

number more accessible and generous: the visual correlation as the characters that touched her life spin nearby but (bar Powell) out of reach before disappearing into the snowfall generalise the sense of how loss lingers, close but never closable. Overall, in enacting how 'these moments given are a gift from time', the filmed accompaniment presents Bush's confirmation, long before her *Director's Cut* reworking, that 'I don't see it as a sad song ... [but] more as a celebration of life' (Ken Bruce Interview, BBC Radio 2, 9 May 2011). With its encompassing mix of mature reflection and direct emotion, 'Moments of Pleasure' constitutes, for this viewer, a highly accomplished section in *TLTC&TC*.

This aesthetic success renders the next scene, a stand-off and chase between Kate and the Woman, all the more unsatisfactory. It is preceded by Kate (again) losing consciousness, then cuts to a music sheet being branded with a cross (inverted, potentially sustaining a witchcraft reading). Recalling 'And So Is Love' with the blackbird (and its symbolic freight) lying on a music score, intratextually this (opaquely) signifies how, by exhibiting valour in her valedictions, Lion-like Kate has regained her heart.

She is awoken by Kemp's Guide shouting through the storm to 'sing for your smile' and performing, one hopes knowingly, the classic-to-the-point-of-clichéd mime trope of 'walking against the wind' (cf. Marcel Marceau's more evident self-parody in *Silent Movie* (Mel Brooks, 1976)). When the Woman re-appears and Kate's snarled 'Bitch, what have you done to me?' is answered by 'Only what was done to me', it is less the blunt emotive and expository dialogue than its delivery that disappoints. The pair's earlier meeting resolved into lip-synched song, where Bush could hold her own with her co-star. Not so here. As they work to outmanoeuvre each other, swapping positions, issuing put-downs, Kate may triumph narratively but not dramatically. Thomson finds that 'Richardson is – typically – sure-footed, but Bush is all at sea, over-acting and over-emphasising'. Thomson too, arguably, overemphasises – this is not a piece, as Richardson demonstrates, necessitating low-key verisimilitude: *The Red Shoes* film also had a highly theatrical delivery. But he is right of Bush that 'Her performance jars' and would have benefited from 'the presence of a director' (2015: 279). That outside influence (Peter Richardson, perhaps?) could have ensured the efficacity of the antagonists' meeting by smoothing out – or at least lessening – their unbalanced acting styles.

There is a further issue as, ideologically, this reprised confrontation problematises a feminist reading of Bush reworking the red shoes myth. She may remove *The Ballad of the Red Shoes*' sexual imperative by forgoing parallels to Vicky's carnival dancing with different men and red-light district wanderings, but devising the Woman as adversary to generate character development and on-screen momentum (cf. lessons learnt filming 'The Dreaming') ultimately confirms that, rather than a single-focused heroic quest where Kate overcomes self-doubts and dismantles patriarchal structures, *TLTC&TC* becomes an internecine same-sex battle where each woman can only save herself at the other's expense. As Withers concedes, 'This is a classically circumscribed liberation for women' (2010: 129): the shoes and the art they connote retain a narrative and symbolic control over the female body and its cultural expression.

Difficulties continue into the next section, where 'Eat the Music' (5.37 minutes, combining album version and 12" intro mix) shows Kate seeking to reclaim her smile aka the Curve. Still chasing the taunting Woman, images of their shuffling feet signal the passage from winter to summer landscapes where filtered camerawork augments a bright and joyous mise-en-scène, for once approximating the saturated technicolor visuals of *The Red Shoes*. Preceded by six dancers sporting the curve symbol on paper strips, the chase dynamic shifts as the Woman becomes fearful and flees down a darkened tunnel, reminiscent of Vicky's nightmare decor.

Kate stays and dances on the fruit-filled floor, the close-up on her feet and laddered tights directly referencing Bush's album front cover. The scene develops into a squishy, fruit-filled, female-dominated communal euphoria that replays a *Zār*, the North African/Middle Eastern multisensory trance-dance ceremony often employed to appease or exorcise spirits from the possessed (Guiley 2009: 277). Now sporting a fruit-patterned dress and her face henna-striped, Kate, with more upbeat echoes of her 'Rubberband Girl' rehearsals with Arnold, is backed by a shamen figure as together they sway into a trance-like state. They seemingly contact spirits who – as indicated by intercutting the symbols flying from the Woman's hand back down the tunnel – return to Kate her smile/'soul', while behind and beside her a chorus line of brightly dressed Black dancers gyrate, sing and experience a similar energy-draining ecstasy (Figure 7.6).

In its favour, this employment of a healing cult is appropriate to the film's narrative momentum, and offers a gendered counterbalance to previous iterations (and Kate's earlier altercation with the Woman). Alongside allowing Kate to enter a state of gleeful dancing, it answers the male chorus on 'The Red Shoes' singing how the titular footwear performs 'a kind of voodoo': here (unlike with Andersen) is a *supportive* religious/mystical

Figure 7.6 The Line, The Cross & The Curve – Music as the Food of Love.

environment. It also adds enriching allusions, both musical and cinematic. Knowledge of *The Red Shoes* album feeds in the reflections on religion voiced on 'Why Should I Love You?', particularly its imagining a less solemn divinity with a laughing Jesus and his healing smile. Moderating this, the fruit on show chimes with *The Red Shoes* film's focus on food, as when Lermontov breakfasts lusciously on a half-melon, sweetened with spoonfuls of sugar. To a ration-hit Britain, this signified not just as the vicarious thrill of conspicuous consumption, but potentially as decadent, orgiastic, even diabolic. As with the Archers, ambivalence remains.

However, 'Eat the Music' also offers up a less profitable double reading as *TLTC&TC*'s optics accentuate the song's inherent problematics. The number exemplifies what, building on Peter Gabriel's promotion of WOMAD and Paul Simon's popularising *Graceland* (1986), became marketed in the late-1980s as 'world music'. It is a label and wider concept that, in an unfavourable aspect of postmodern practice, can smack of exploitative cultural appropriation and the asymmetrical power relations of global capitalism (Frith 2000: 305–322). Here the visuals exacerbate these issues both for positioning and props. Relegating the 16 Black dancers to background/marginal positions while Kate sways front and centre undermines their narrative import – the co-opting of their religious practices for a White woman's personal/mythological 'soul searching' only intensifies the sense of unequal power dynamics. Ron Moy blithely dismissed the sequence as resembling a 'commercial for mango smoothies' (2007: 104), but the reductionistic play with 'voodoo' practices risks accusations of perpetuating racialised stereotypes similar, for example, to those 'betrayed' in the differently genred and gendered James Bond vehicle, *Live and Let Die* (Guy Hamilton, 1973). For these dancers then to cavort while holding watermelons on their heads evinces an insensitivity to racist tropes surpassing Bush's clumsiness with class depictions.[11] This is not just a retrospective reading: these scenes were reshot/excised as they were deemed too provocative for US release (Thomson 2015: 277).

An anti-climactic conclusion follows. After this Dionysian dance piece, when Kate awakens (from her third fainting) to find the three symbols in her hand and the red shoes on the Woman's feet, their final face-off ends when the Woman falls back and breaks the mirror, releasing a torrent of water (reminiscent of the album cover background) that buries her in a mound of rubble. 'Hello,' the Guide says (bathetically), approaching the Woman's still-dancing feet, as Kate returns to the studio and the electricity sparks back into life. A reprise of 'The Red Shoes' (3.57 minutes) takes us into the final credits, including, before a brief return to red shoes dancing, a final 'Thanks to' that includes Michael Powell.

Evaluation

How finally to assess *TLTC&TC*? Bonnie Gordon posits that Bush's 'technological proficiency' helps her to rewrite myth in *The Red Shoes*: 'With it [she] exhibits mastery and control, precisely what the fairy tale takes away from its protagonist' (2005: 42). Even if such 'mastery' is accepted for her musical production (debatable given her original intentions and later re-recordings), can the judgement hold for Bush the filmmaker? Delaying the album to coincide with the release of *TLTC&TC* can be explained as a studio move to maximise income from synergistic exhibition strategies. But Bush now exercised considerable autonomy and their simultaneous release can equally indicate an authoritative artistic move, permitting album and film to offer mutual enrichment when read with and against each other, their dynamic presenting a late-twentieth-century re-imagining of the fairy-tale format.

However, as Noël Carroll has posited, allusive works must also function independently, and this is again debatable with *TLTC&TC*. It is not that the film is unduly pleased with itself (far from it, as evidenced by Bush's self-castigations). Rather, it can be argued that, where the album intermittently struggles with influence and allusion, Bush's film, with one further level of intertextuality, is insufficiently transmuted into a separate and self-standing artwork; it is arguably too full of its own concept, too 'meta' to mean or matter sufficiently to the general consumer. When discussed, it has been criticised for instancing an artist/auteur 'over-reaching': here was Bush taking on too much, too quickly, in a solipsistic project that would have benefitted from more objective perspectives.

Life did not imitate art with *TLTC&TC*. Rather than returning from the experience to fulfil Campbell's paradigm and 'bestow boons' with further artworks, Bush retreated into what Lermontov scornfully dismissed as 'the doubtful comforts of human love'. For 30 years *TLTC&TC* was largely erased from Bush's back catalogue and faded from public and critical consciousness. This, I would contend, is unwarranted and, as noted, appears to be changing. In his 2005 monograph on Powell and Pressburger's *The Red Shoes*, Mark Connelly assessed the legacy of this cinema 'phenomenon' – 'It has spawned thousands of ballerinas, numerous video releases and even a Broadway musical version' – but made no mention of Bush's album or accompanying film (2005: 88). More recent studies, however, list Bush as an artist who 'answered the film's challenge' (Hutchinson 2023: 102–103), and 'brings out the erotic charge of the Archers' film' (Warner 2023: 168). Such a 'wilderness period' is not unknown for artistic creations. In his pioneering *A Mirror for England*, Raymond Durgnat opined that the Powell–Pressburger film suffered the fate common to artworks that show 'a new stylistic flexibility of approach': 'Instantly praised, they appear infuriatingly pretentious for some years afterwards, before finding their own level, which is an honourable one' (1970: 210). This chapter concludes that Bush's own reworking of *The Red Shoes* (praised at least on its opening night) is, if not a cinema 'phenomenon', due a similar – and honourable – re-evaluation.

Notes

1 On contemporaneous press responses to *The Red Shoes*, see Connelly (2005): 68–75.
2 *The Red Shoes* continues to exercise a strong cross-genre influence: e.g. *Black Swan* (Darren Aronofsky, 2010), *Suspiria* (Luca Guadagnino, 2018) and *Barbie* (Greta Gerwig, 2023).
3 On Beck vetoing his performance, see Glynn (2022): 24. It was restored for the film's July 2023 4K re-release.
4 There are no extant press reviews for *TLTC&TC* in the files of London's BFI Library.

5 For instance, *TLTC&TC* was screened on 10 June 2014 at the Holocene, Portland, Oregon, supported by modern dance interpretations of Bush's music. https://www.facebook.com/events/1475132096053262/ [accessed 8 January 2024].
6 Similar to Bush, Potter lamented that *The Gold Diggers* was 'the greatest learning experience of my life ... But I think the film was a monumental failure' (Scott MacDonald, 'Interview with Sally Potter'. *Camera Obscura*, 10, 35, May 1995: 204).
7 Stephen Troussé indicatively (and condescendingly) termed Bush 'the mad woman in the attic of British pop, a last spectral link to that Old Weird England' ('The Arc Ascending', *Uncut*, 103, December 2005: 98). Conversely, a Bush-inspired anthology of stories is proudly entitled *Let the Weirdness In: A Tribute to Kate Bush*, Ed. E. St. Jones, Louisiana: Heads Dance Press, 2022.
8 'Shoedance', a 10-minute dance mix issued as a CD supplement to 'The Red Shoes' single, also featured dialogue from *TLTC&TC*. It is the only credited work from producer Karl Blagan, assumed to be a pseudonym for Bush herself.
9 Without imputing direct influence, this alternate dimension is not dissimilar from the Upside Down in *Stranger Things*.
10 One allusion: Kate passing through a window into a star-filled sky potentially references the opening sequence to CBS's *The Twilight Zone*.
11 A spirited (though to this reader unconvincing) defence that, for narrative, symbolical and mythological integrity, 'This scene *should* be read for its dubious racial imagery and the way it bluntly exoticises blackness' is offered by Withers (2010: 132).

8 Conclusion
Kate Bush and the Whole Story

In his review of Kate Bush's album *The Dreaming*, Colin Irwin lauded passages of 'both beauty and anguish, poignancy and eeriness' before admitting that:

> I'm still not entirely sure what the hell's going on or what it's all about, but the puzzle's intriguing enough to entice you back until you unravel it. It's the sort of album that makes me want to kidnap the artist and demand the explanation and inspiration behind each track.
>
> (*Melody Maker*, 11 September 1982)

Bush's work can have this effect: an enjoyment of the melodic control and sonic palette but, for those where intentionality matters, a vaguely frustrating sense that full comprehension lies (just) out of reach. This monograph, obeying ethical research principles and forgoing the kidnap option, has drawn on Noël Carroll's notions of dual address and endeavoured to offer an (inevitably partial) answer to such responses for greater understanding, thereby adding an 'informed' level of explanation to the artist's sustained use of allusion.

Kate Bush and the Moving Image presents an interdisciplinary study, overlapping with biography, pop musicology, stardom, performance, and gender studies, but focusing on a particular frame of reference. It understands that inspiration for any creative endeavour is an amalgam of lived and learnt experiences, and recognises that Bush's work is peppered with allusions to historical, scientific, and literary sources. The book does not dwell, though, on these sources, or presume to venture into Bush's religio-philosophical-mystical explorations: it leaves to others to explicate her references to George Gurdjieff ('Them Heavy People') and to a Catholic God (multiple). Nor does it detail the plethora of musical influences ranging from Anne Briggs to Ziggy Stardust via Frederick Delius and Pink Floyd. Instead it looks at a specific area of influence, deemed most pervasive in its allusive weight, namely Bush's recourse to works of film and television.

Such intermedial linkages have been noted elsewhere. In his *Melody Maker* review, Irwin conjectured on influences and concluded that 'Personally I reckon the girl watches too many B-movies'. Bush biographer Graeme Thomson more fulsomely declared that:

> film and video was always likely to prove irresistible to Bush. A woman who had frequently found cinema a direct source of inspiration in her writing, who often approached composition in a highly visual way and is acutely aware of the importance of projecting a compelling image, she was bound to recognise the medium as an outlet for many of her ideas.
>
> (2015: 265)

This study has sought to substantiate such pronouncements through its detailed textual readings. It undertakes an investigation and interrogation of how these examples of the moving image have impacted on her musical lyrics, promotional videos and entries into filmmaking, both explicitly via direct reference and/or supportive statement, and implicitly/potentially through more oblique access, cogent critical responses and/or academic exegesis.

The theoretical underpinning to this study has been the reading of Bush's artistic practice as primarily postmodern in nature. This again is not intended as a particularly original pronouncement. Reynolds and Press cite Bush as (like Madonna) employing a strategy that 'celebrates female imagery and iconography, but in a more provisional, postmodern way', one that 'plays with cultural representations of femininity' (1995: 233, 289). For Christopher Knowles, 'Bush's mix of musical virtuosity and assertive individualism altered the DNA of the postmodern chanteuse' (2010: 123). This book proposes an equivalent assessment, evidencing the repeated employment of film and television influences as core elements in Bush's advancement of that postmodern DNA.

Another important aspect of *Kate Bush and the Moving Image* has been its dual focus on Bush as performer *and* auteur, notably her move towards director of her promo videos and film venture: this hopefully contributes to current re-examinations of women's agency in the arts. It places Bush at the nexus of several creative industries – music, video, television, film – and considers her agency not just as a recording musician but also as a significant performer and director in the contexts of the formative years of the pop video/promo film, pushing against the dictates of acceptable discourse and duration, and thereby expanding the format's creative contours. Not everything she produced can be considered aesthetically (or commercially) successful, and examples of and explanations for such works duly feature. Even here, though, one can offer a (partial) positive in acknowledging the willingness to experiment and (at times) to overreach/fail, much like her early idol David Bowie in his musical and film ventures.

This artistic practice and its varying results have been examined over three avenues of production. Part 1 examined how the influence, evident or oblique, of film and television on Bush's musical compositions could be traced through their titles, lyrics and narrative progression. Her debut hit, 'Wuthering Heights', was shown as indicative in functioning not as a deferential cross-media adaptation but rather a reimagining or 'parallel text' wherein Cathy Earnshaw/Linton was empowered with fresh agency and self-narration. Similar reworkings employed not so much Irwin's B-movie influences but mainstream and art-house productions by canonical directors like Francis Ford Coppola, Walt Disney, Stanley Kubrick and Ken Russell. Evidencing Bush's own agency, this first part also explored the varying results of her bespoke soundtrack compositions, wide-ranging in their cinematic accomplishment (even their inclusion) but most achieved in the extractable and reusable 'This Woman's Work'. Bush's involvement was shown, just once, to extend to on-screen acting, where her performance in *The Comic Strip Presents* episode *Les Dogs* revealed a strong screen presence and comic potential never, sadly, repeated.

Part 2 examined Bush's work in promotional videos. Rob Young proclaims Bush musically 'intriguing' because of 'the way she harnesses modern electronics and studio techniques to traditional instrumental textures and a lyrical sensibility that … obliquely draws on the ballad canon' (2011: 569). Visually, it is argued that Bush similarly harnesses the burgeoning pop video genre to a grammar that heavily draws on the (western) cinematic and televisual canon. Tracing allusions to the moving image in her work here exhibits both continuity and change. The videos spanning her 'Wuthering Heights' debut through to her latest (to date) 'And Dream of Sheep (Live)' consistently foreground Bush's charismatic star presence and feature her performances as a persona in unconventional, liminal states. Concurrently, they develop in sophistication and ambition from interpretive dance pieces (e.g. 'The Man with the Child in His Eyes') to socially conscious enactments of ecological disaster ('Breathing') and technological dysfunction ('Deeper Understanding'). The shift from an overwrought youthful choreography, evidenced as divisive in audience engagement, to a mature stillness, evaluated as Beckettian in probing the reach of the visible, parallels Bush's move to full agency and authorial control in this domain.

The extended case study undertaken in Part 3 shows this allusive modus operandi to be both extrapolated and pierced by Bush's most source-signalled album, *The Red Shoes*, and the extended film she made to accompany its release, *The Line, The Cross & the Curve*. Extrapolation is evidenced ideologically in the attempted reworking of a patriarchal mythology to favour a feminist perspective, and aesthetically via the enrichment attained by revisiting allusions across tracks, scenes, even the two media. The play here with images, symbols and themes is clearly derived principally from Powell and Pressburger, but is shown also to pull in previously employed allusions such as Alfred Hitchcock and Jacques Tourneur (thus providing a compendium of Bush's practice to that point), and to open out towards contemporary artists including Sally Potter and Wim Wenders (thus pointing to future preoccupations). It is adjudged as pierced because, though still encased in a wider structure of allusion, in places both album and film allow a rare excursion into the openly autobiographical. While not intending to decry 'honest and open' artistic expression or imply a communicative hierarchy (Robert Lowell can be appreciated equally with T.S. Eliot), in Bush's case this shift of expressive mode, especially on *The Red Shoes*, can lead to instances of (generally adjudged) aesthetic weakness, indicative of how, without the conduit and thematic resonance of references to other works, her writing can slip into the musically indifferent and lyrically/narratively opaque. Not always, though: 'Moments of Pleasure' offers an accomplished dramatic excursion, a raid on the personal rather than a construct for it, and the opportunity to share a brief intimacy with Bush as a grieving, growing woman.

This (personal, emotive) response exposes a potential tension in tracing the allusive matrix in Bush's work. Bush is an exploratory artist, delving deep into her personal and cultural experiences and expressing herself via objective correlatives, whereas *Kate Bush and the Moving Image* is an explanatory volume, bringing many of these influences out into the light, exposing and explicating her subjective feelings and philosophy. If the allusive approach is read (amongst its assets) as allowing Bush to articulate intimate desires while constructing a sense of distance, thereby offering psychological, emotional and even social protection, then dispassionately decoding such a strategy could be criticised as working against the grain of authorial intent. I would (of course) contest it does not. While such an exegetical undertaking necessarily entails a process of deconstruction, even arguably a sense of diminishment in reducing tightly knit and complex utterances to discrete strands, there is no implication that Bush's 'music of allusion' is in itself restricting, a less inviting/welcoming form that the more open and 'confessional' form of singer-songwriting. Far from it: (Kate Bush can be appreciated equally with Joni Mitchell). Rather than a schematic either/or, it is argued that, through her pervasive use of allusion, Bush is not withholding but *generalising* her experiences. Rather than becoming a single point of negative capability, she employs a 'subversive performativity' (Gordon 2005: 46), operating (again like Bowie) as a chameleon able, in sound and vision, to become anyone or anything she wants to be, ranging from a Norman Bates-style murderer ('Mother Stands for Comfort') to a Joan of Arc-style martyr ('Joanni'), a ruminative drowning woman ('The Ninth Wave') to a braying mule-child ('Get Out of My House'). Singing, performing and directing from and into multiple identities and personae, experience is turned into another point of view, life is transmuted, giving all permission to find therein their own deeper understanding. Kate Bush and the listener/viewer thus mutually benefit from her creative use of the moving image.

Appendix: Kate Bush's Desert Island Films

Interview from March 1983

There can't be many men who would turn down the opportunity of rescuing Kate Bush from a desert island. However, Kate might just be a little reluctant to get back to civilisation.

'Being stuck there could be an idyllic time,' she says. 'I've always enjoyed working alone, even as a kid, and I can collect all my thoughts together then. But the prospect of being there with my favorite films is exciting, because I love the cinema and rarely get the chance to visit it because of my work. So I'd go to town on my selection.'

Kagemusha [1980]

'Not a lot of people have heard of this one, but it's by the Japanese director Akira Kurosawa. I just happen to think that this is one of his best. It was a toss-up between this and his *Seven Samurai* [1954], which is a tremendously atmospheric picture. However, I think this one wins the day.'

Psycho [1960]

'As there wouldn't be a shower within thousands of miles ... or a motel ... I'd feel quite safe having this along with me. Of course it scares me silly, and the fact that it's in black and white only adds to the terror, but Anthony Perkins is so marvellous in it. It's one of those films I can watch lots of times, even though I know the ending.'

Time Bandits [1980]

'This is the kind of film that'll be around for years – like the Disney ones. When Terry Gilliam and Michael Palin of the Monty Python team got together on this they must have been inspired, because it appeals to kids and adults alike. The story is so original and seems to incorporate just about everything from pantomime, fairy tales, drama ... the whole show.'

Don't Look Now *[1973]*

'Donald Sutherland I can always watch – he's got such a wry sense of humour. Ever since I saw him in *M*A*S*H* [Robert Altman, 1970] I became a fan. And yet in this film there's no humour at all. It's real creepy and has a terrifying climax. But there's such a lot to be observed in the relationship between Donald Sutherland and Julie Christie that you don't get tired of it.'

Night of the Demon *[1957]*

'This is an oldie, if the fifties can be described as old. *Night of the Demon* is one of the better horror films from that period, which really keeps you on the edge of your seat without frightening you out of it. It's about a secret ancient inscription of the rune symbols at Stonehenge. Whoever holds a certain piece of paper with them written on incites the wrath of the demons. Very exciting.'

Barry Lyndon *[Stanley Kubrick, 1975]*

'Not too much to say about this film, except that I love the story and the whole atmosphere of the film. It's just a picture that moves me emotionally.'

Notorious *[1946]*

'Marvellous Hitchcock stuff. Really vintage and one of the classics with Ingrid Bergman and Cary Grant. It's that build-up of mystery that fascinates me.'

Pinocchio *[1940]*

'This film just goes on forever; it's timeless. I saw it when I was a kid and I go to see it whenever it comes on the circuit. Magical! I love fairy stories anyway.'

To Kill a Mockingbird *[Robert Mulligan, 1963]*

'I read the book, then saw the film, and I wasn't disappointed. It's the story that appeals most here. Just a marvellous film.'

Appendix: Kate Bush's Desert Island Films

The Empire Strikes Back *[Irvin Kershner, 1980]*

'Working this lot out, I've realized what contrasting tastes I've got in films. But here, I think that the sequel to *Star Wars* is better than its predecessor. There was always the risk that it would be some kind of anti-climax, but it goes beyond expectations.'

(John Kercher, 'Kate's Desert Island Films', *Popular Video*, March 1983)

Videography

Music Videos

1978 Wuthering Heights [red dress] d. Nick Abson
Wuthering Heights [white dress] d. Keith MacMillan
The Man with the Child in His Eyes d. Keith MacMillan
Hammer Horror d. Keith MacMillan

1979 Wow d. Keith MacMillan
Them Heavy People d. Keith MacMillan

1980 Breathing d. Keith MacMillan
Babooshka d. Keith MacMillan
Delius (Song of Summer) d. Keith MacMillan
Army Dreamers d. Keith MacMillan

1981 Sat in Your Lap d. Brian Wiseman

1982 The Dreaming d. Paul Henry
There Goes a Tenner d. Paul Henry
Suspended in Gaffa d. Brian Wiseman

1985 Running Up That Hill d. David Garfath
Cloudbusting d. Julian Doyle

1986 Hounds of Love d. Kate Bush
The Big Sky d. Kate Bush
Don't Give Up [with Peter Gabriel] d. Kevin Godley, Lol Creme
Experiment IV d. Kate Bush

1989 The Sensual World d. Kate Bush, Peter Richardson
This Woman's Work d. Kate Bush

1990 Love and Anger d. Kate Bush

1991 Rocket Man d. Kate Bush

1993 Rubberband Girl d. Kate Bush
Eat the Music d. Kate Bush
Moments of Pleasure d. Kate Bush

1994 The Red Shoes d. Kate Bush
The Man I Love [with Larry Adler] d. Kevin Godley
And So Is Love d. Kate Bush

2005 King of the Mountain d. Jimmy Murakami

2011 Deeper Understanding d. Kate Bush
Wild Man Segment d. Kate Bush
Mistraldespair d. Kate Bush

2012 Eider Falls at Lake Tahoe d. Kate Bush

2016 And Dream of Sheep (Live) d. David Garfath

VHS Video Albums

November 1981

Live at Hammersmith Odeon (+ Betamax)
   Moving; Them Heavy People; Violin; Strange Phenomena; Hammer Horror; Don't Push Your Foot on the Heartbrake; Wow; Feel It; Kite; James and the Cold Gun; Oh England My Lionheart; Wuthering Heights.

November 1983

The Single File (+ Betamax, Laserdisc and CED Disc)
   Wuthering Heights; The Man with the Child in His Eyes; Hammer Horror; Wow; Them Heavy People; Breathing; Babooshka; Army Dreamers; Sat in Your Lap; The Dreaming; Suspended in Gaffa; There Goes a Tenner.

June 1986

The Hair of the Hound (+ Betamax and Laserdisc)
   Running Up That Hill; Hounds of Love; The Big Sky; Cloudbusting.

November 1986

The Whole Story (+ Laserdisc and Video CD)
 Wuthering Heights; Cloudbusting; The Man with the Child in His Eyes; Breathing; Wow [alternate video]; Hounds of Love; Running Up That Hill; Army Dreamers; Sat in Your Lap; Experiment IV; The Dreaming; Babooshka; The Big Sky

February 1990

The Sensual World – The Videos (+ Laserdisc)
 Interview for VH1; The Sensual World; Love and Anger; This Woman's Work

May 1994

The Line, The Cross & The Curve (+ Laserdisc)
 Rubberband Girl; And So Is Love; The Red Shoes; Lily; The Red Shoes (instrumental); Moments of Pleasure; Eat the Music; The Red Shoes

Bibliography

Andersen, H.C. (1983) *The Complete Illustrated Stories.* London: Chancellor Press.
Anderson, J. (2022) 'The Videos'. *Uncut: The Ultimate Music Guide. Kate Bush.* July.
Aspinall, S. (1983) 'Women, Realism and Reality in British Films, 1943–53', in J. Curran and V. Porter (Eds.) *British Cinema History.* London: Weidenfeld and Nicolson.
Beckett, S. (1990) *The Complete Dramatic Works.* London: Faber and Faber.
Binnie, S. (2016) *Feeling Like a Number One: The Unofficial 1980s Top of the Pops Guidebook.* Morrisville, NC: Lulu Press.
Bordwell, D., Staiger, J. and Thompson, K. (1985) *The Classical Hollywood Cinema: Film Style and Mode of Production to 1960.* New York: Columbia University Press.
Buckley, D. (2005) *Strange Fascination – David Bowie: The Definitive Story.* London: Virgin.
Burton, A. and Chibnall, S. (2013) *Historical Dictionary of British Cinema.* Lanham, MD: Scarecrow Press.
Butler, J. (2014) 'Album Art and Posters: The Psychedelic Interplay of Rock Art and Art Rock', in T. Shephard and A. Leonard (Eds.) *The Routledge Companion to Music and Visual Culture.* Abingdon: Routledge.
Calavito, M. (2007) 'MTV Aesthetics at the Movies: Interrogating a Film Criticism Fallacy'. *Journal of Film and Video,* 59, 3, Fall.
Camon, A. (2000) '*The Godfather* and the Mythology of Mafia', in N. Browne (Ed.) *Francis Ford Coppola's The Godfather Trilogy.* Cambridge: Cambridge University Press.
Campbell, J. (1968) *The Hero with a Thousand Faces* 2nd edn. Princeton: Princeton University Press.
Campbell, J. (1988) *The Power of Myth.* New York: Doubleday.
Carroll, N. (1998) *Interpreting the Moving Image.* Cambridge: Cambridge University Press.
Caston, E. (2020) *British Music Videos, 1966–2016: Genre, Authenticity and Art.* Edinburgh: Edinburgh University Press.

Cawood, I. (2016) '"Don't Let Me Go! Hold Me Down!": Inspiration, Voice and Image in Kate Bush's *Hounds of Love*'. *Popular Music*, 35, 1.
Christie, I. (1994) *Arrows of Desire: The Films of Michael Powell and Emeric Pressburger* 2nd edn. London: Faber and Faber.
Christie, T.A. (2012) *John Hughes and Eighties Cinema: Teenage Hopes and American Dreams* 3rd edn. Maidstone: Crescent Moon.
Connelly, M. (2005) *The Red Shoes*. London: I.B. Tauris.
Connor, S. (1989) *Postmodernist Culture: An Introduction to Theories of the Contemporary*. Oxford: Basil Blackwell.
Dahl, N. (2016) 'Kate Bush's Cinema of Sound'. *Dazed*, 23 November. https://www.dazeddigital.com/music/article/33816/1/kate-bush-s-cinema-of-sound [accessed 18 February 2024].
Davidson, H. (2011) 'Sex and Sin: The Magic of Red Shoes', in G. Riella and P. McNeil (Eds.) *Shoes: A History from Sandals to Sneakers*. Oxford: Berg.
Diliberto, J. (1990) 'Kate Bush's Theatre of the Senses'. *Musician*, 135, February.
Dixon, I. and Black, B. (2022) *I Am Not a Film Star: David Bowie as Actor*. London: Bloomsbury Academic.
Donnelly, K.J. (1994) 'Altered Status: A Review of Music in Postmodern Cinema and Culture', in S. Earnshaw (Ed.) *Postmodern Surroundings*. Amsterdam: Rodopi.
Doyle, T. (2005) 'Weak? Frail? Mentally Unstable? Fuck off!' *Mojo*, 145, December.
Doyle, T. (2022) *Running Up That Hill: 50 Visions of Kate Bush*. London: Nine Eight Books.
Durgnat, R. (1970) *A Mirror for England: British Movies from Austerity to Affluence*. London: Faber and Faber.
Forrester, C. (2021) 'Artist to Auteur: The Cinema of Kate Bush'. *Film Cred*. https://film-cred.com/kate-bush-cinema-the-red-shoes/ [accessed 17 December 2023].
Frith, S. (2000) 'The Discourse of World Music', in G. Born and D. Hesmondhalgh (Eds.) *Western Music and Its Others: Difference, Representation and Appropriation in Music*. Berkeley: University of California Press.
Glancy, M. (2003) *The 39 Steps: A British Film Guide*. London: I.B. Tauris.
Glynn, S. (2022) *David Bowie and Film: Hooked to the Silver Screen*. London: Palgrave Macmillan.
Goodall, M., Good, J. and Goodall, W. (2009) *Crash Cinema: Representation in Film*. Cambridge: Cambridge Scholars Publishing.
Gordon, B. (2005) 'Kate Bush's Subversive Shoes'. *Women and Music: A Journal of Gender and Culture*, 9.
Graham, M. (1991) *Blood Memory: An Autobiography*. New York: Doubleday.
Guiley, R.E. (2009) *The Encyclopedia of Demons and Demonology*. New York: Facts on File.
Hasted, N. (2022) 'The Red Shoes'. *Uncut: The Ultimate Music Guide. Kate Bush*. July.

Hazette, V. (2015) *Wuthering Heights on Film and Television: A Journey Across Time and Cultures*. Bristol: Intellect.

Hearn, M. and Barnes, A. (2007) *The Hammer Story: The Authorised History of Hammer Films* 2nd edn. London: Titan Books.

Holmes, D. and Ingram, R. (1998) *François Truffaut*. Manchester: Manchester University Press.

Honess Roe, A. (2013) *Animated Documentary*. London: Palgrave Macmillan.

Hornbeck, E.J. (2017) 'Who's Afraid of the Big Bad Wolf?: Domestic Violence in *The Shining*'. *Feminist Studies*, 42, 3.

Hutcheon, L. (1988) *A Poetics of Postmodernism: History, Theory, Fiction*. New York and London: Routledge.

Hutchinson, P. (2023) *The Red Shoes*. London: BFI and Bloomsbury.

Irwin, C. (1980) 'Paranoia and Passion of the Kate Inside'. *Melody Maker*, 4 October.

Jameson, F. (1991) *Postmodernism, or the Cultural Logic of Late Capitalism*. Durham, NC: Duke University Press.

Jameson, F. (1992) *The Geopolitical Aesthetic: Cinema and Space in the World System*. London: BFI.

Jeffries, S. (2022) *Everything, All the Time, Everywhere: How We Became Postmodern*. London: Verso.

Jones, N. (2018) 'Elgar and Delius', in P. Fryer (Ed.) *The Composer on Screen: Essays on Classical Music Biopics*. Jefferson, NC: McFarland.

Jovanovic, R. (2005) *Kate Bush: The Biography*. London: Portrait.

Jowett, L. and Abbott, S. (2013) *TV Horror: Investigating the Dark Side of the Small Screen*. London: I.B. Tauris.

Kalush, W. and Sloman, L. (2006) *The Secret Life of Houdini: The Making of America's First Superhero*. London: Simon and Schuster.

Kline, S. (Ed.) (1999) *George Lucas Interviews*. Jackson, MI: University Press of Mississippi.

Knowles, C. (2010) *The Secret History of Rock'n'Roll: The Mysterious Roots of Modern Music*. Berkeley CA: Viva Editions.

Kuhn, A. (1994) *Women's Pictures: Feminism and Cinema* 2nd edn. London: Verso.

Kynaston, D. (2008) *Austerity Britain, 1945–51*. London: Bloomsbury.

Lamb, B. (2020) *You're Nicked: Investigating British Television Police Series*. Manchester: Manchester University Press.

Lindsay, M. (2012) 'Thirty Years On: The Dreaming by Kate Bush'. *The Quietus*, 11 September. https://thequietus.com/articles/09945-kate-bush-the-dreaming [accessed 5 March 2024].

Lindsay, M. (2023) 'Passion Always Wins: Kate Bush in 1978'. *The Quietus*, 13 June. https://thequietus.com/articles/33040-kate-bush-1978 [accessed 25 January 2024].

Macdonald, K. (1994) *Emeric Pressburger: The Life and Death of a Screenwriter*. London: Faber and Faber.

Maltin, L. (1987) *Of Mice and Magic: A History of American Animated Cartoons* rev. edn. New York: Plume.

Mendelsohn, F. (2008) *Rhetorics of Fantasy*. Middletown: Wesleyan University Press.

Marks, P. (2009) *Terry Gilliam*. Manchester: Manchester University Press.

Marks, P. (2019) '"Are These Feelings Ever Real?" Intimacy and Authenticity in Spike Jonze's *Her*', in K. Wilkins and W. Moss-Wellington (Eds.) *ReFocus: The Films of Spike Jonze*. Edinburgh: Edinburgh University Press.

Martin, P. (2022) 'Hounds of Love'. *Uncut: The Ultimate Music Guide. Kate Bush*. July.

Masco, J. (2006) *The Nuclear Borderlands: The Manhattan Project in Post-Cold War New Mexico*. Princeton: Princeton University Press.

McMullan, A. (2010) *Performing Embodiment in Samuel Beckett's Drama*. London: Routledge.

Mendelssohn, J. (2004) *Waiting for Kate Bush*. London: Omnibus Press.

Moor, A. (2005) *Powell and Pressburger: A Cinema of Magic Spaces*. London: I.B. Tauris.

Moy, R. (2007) *Kate Bush and Hounds of Love*. Hampshire: Ashgate Publishing.

Oliver, M. (2020) *Household Horror: Cinematic Fear and the Secret Life of Everyday Objects*. Bloomington: Indiana University Press.

Perrott, L. (2024) *David Bowie and the Art of Music Video*. London: Bloomsbury.

Powell, M. (1992) *A Life in Movies*. London: Faber and Faber.

Powers, A. (2022) 'Kate Bush: The Power of Strange Things'. *Archive on* 4. BBC Radio 4, 1 October.

Ramon, A. (2022) 'Lost and Found: *The Line, the Cross & the Curve*'. *Sight and Sound*, 32, 7, September.

Reed, K. (2023) *David Bowie and the Moving Image: A Standing Cinema*. London: Bloomsbury Academic.

Reinholtz, E.L. (2012) 'Supper, Slapstick and Social Class: Dinner as Machine in the Silent Films of Buster Keaton', in A.L. Bower (Ed.) *Reel Food: Essays on Food and Film*. New York and London: Routledge.

Reynolds, S. (2016) *Shock and Awe: Glam Rock and its Legacy from the Seventies to the Twenty-First Century*. London: Faber and Faber.

Reynolds, S. and Press, J. (1995) *The Sex Revolts: Gender, Rebellion and Rock'n'Roll*. London: Serpent's Tail.

Sangster, J. and Condon, P. (2005) *TV Heaven*. London: Collins.

Schoonmaker, T., Von Bagh, P. and Durgnat, R. (2003) 'Midnight Sun Film Festival', in D. Lazar (Ed.) *Michael Powell Interviews*. Jackson: University of Mississippi Press.

Sergeant, A. (2005) *British Cinema: A Critical History*. London: BFI.

Shaw, F. (2008) 'Many Happy Days'. *New England Review*, 29, 4.

Sheil, T. (2008) '*The Red Shoes*', in S. Barrow and J. White (Eds.) *Fifty Key British Films*. London: Routledge.

Shuker, R. (1994) *Key Concepts in Popular Music*. London: Routledge.

Sinyard, N. (1991) *The Films of Nicolas Roeg*. London: Letts.

Bibliography

Sinyard, N. (2000) *Jack Clayton*. Manchester: Manchester University Press.
Strank, W. (2014) *Twist Endings: Reinterpreting Film Endings*. Cologne: Schüren.
Straw, W. (2018) 'Music Video in Its Contexts: 30 Years Later'. *Volume! La revue des musiques populaires*, 14, 2.
Strick, J.E. (2015) *Wilhelm Reich, Biologist*. Cambridge, MA: Harvard University Press.
Thomson, G. (2015) *Under the Ivy: The Life and Music of Kate Bush* new edn. London: Omnibus Press.
Tibbitts, J.C. (2005) *Composers in the Movies: Studies in Musical Biography*. New Haven: Yale University Press.
Tremblay, J.-T. (2022) *Breathing Aesthetics*. Durham: Duke University Press.
Turner, G. (1999) *Film as Social Practice* 3rd edn. London: Routledge.
Van der Kiste, J. (2021) *Kate Bush: Song by Song*. London: Fonthill Press.
Warner, M. (2023) '*The Red Shoes*', in N. Morris and C. Smith (Eds.) *The Cinema of Powell and Pressburger*. London: BFI.
Wells, P. (1998) *Understanding Animation*. London: Routledge.
Wells, P. (2004) 'On Being an Impish God', in D. Sterritt and L. Rhodes (Eds.) *Terry Gilliam: Interviews*. Jackson: University of Minnesota Press.
Wells, P. (2020) 'The Disruptive Metamorphoses of an Impish God', in K. Egan and J.A. Weinstock (Eds.) *And Now for Something Completely Different: Critical Approaches to Monty Python*. Edinburgh: Edinburgh University Press.
White, S. (2014) 'A Surface Collaboration: Hitchcock and Performance', in T. Leitch and L. Poague (Eds.) *A Companion to Alfred Hitchcock*. Chichester: Wiley-Blackwell.
Withers, D.M. (2010) *Adventures in Kate Bush and Theory*. Bristol: HammerOn Press.
Young, R. (2011) *Electric Eden: Unearthing Britain's Visionary Music*. London: Faber and Faber.
Young, R. (2021) *The Magic Box: Viewing Britain Through the Rectangular Window*. London: Faber and Faber.
Young, R. (2022) 'Director's Cut'. *Uncut: The Ultimate Music Guide. Kate Bush*. July.
Zipes, J. (2005) *Hans Christian Andersen: The Misunderstood Storyteller*. New York and London: Routledge.

Index

39 Steps, The 64–65
50 Words for Snow 4, 76, 97n4, 99

Abominable Snowman, The 77
Abson, Nick 19
Achilléos, Chris 50
Adler, Larry 61n7
Adventures of Prince Achmed, The 78
Aerial (album) 72, 73, 85
'Aerial' (song) 82n11
Aivazovsky, Ivan 33
Alice in Wonderland 108
Alien 31, 59, 71
Allen, Kevin 43
Allsopp, Robert, 78
Always 92
American in Paris, An 103
'Among Angels' 97n4
Amos, Tori 4
'And Dream of Sheep' 79
'And Dream of Sheep (Live)' 79–81, 118, 127
'And So Is Love' 90, 95, 96, 97n8, 104, 112, 119
Andersen, Hans Christian 12, 89, 92, 93, 95, 99–101, 103, 112, 114, 117, 118, 120
Anderson, Brett 61n1
Andrews, Julie 56, 66
Andy Pandy 97n1
Angels 92
Apocalypse Now 30
Ariel 85
'Army Dreamers' 25, 51–52, 55, 61n6, 112, 117

Arnold, Stewart 56, 90, 105, 110–111, 113, 120
Arsenic and Old Lace 23
Ask Aspel 35n6
'Astronomer's Tale, The' 82n13
Auric, Georges 27

'Babooshka' 50, 51, 61n4
Bacharach, Burt 29
Back to the Future 60
Barbie 123n2
Baretta 24
Barratt, John 85, 97n1
Barrie, J.M. 22, 42, 99
Barry, John 37
Barry Lyndon 131
Bassey, Shirley 37
Battleship Potemkin 59
Baum, Frank L. 108
'Be Kind to My Mistakes' 38–39, 40, 46n1
Beatles, The 3
Beck, Jeff 88, 95, 103, 123n3
Beckett, Samuel 11, 75, 80–81, 82n15, 117, 127
'Before the Dawn' (residency) 6, 79–80, 81, 82n11, 82n13, 82n14, 94
Before the Dawn (album) 80, 81
Benn, Tony 42
'Between a Man and a Woman' 34–35
Bierce, Ambrose 44
Big Little Lies 13n1
'Big Sky, The' 66–67, 69, 94, 117

'Big Stripey Lie' 94, 97
Biggles 69
Black Corridor, The 94
Black Narcissus 86
Black Swan 123n2
Block, Robert 33
Blood of a Poet, The 109
Bogart, Humphrey 29, 50
Bond, James 20, 21, 37, 122
Bones 13n1
Book of Dreams, A 57, 59
Bourne, Matthew 100
Bowie, David 3, 4–7, 8, 13n3, 13n4, 13n5, 17, 36n9, 37, 50, 54, 71–72, 87, 103, 110, 127, 129
Brando, Marlon 34
Brazil (film) 38, 40, 44, 56, 57, 58, 69, 78, 91
'Brazil' (song) 38
'Breathing' 5, 51, 52–55, 61n8, 67, 117, 127
Bride Wore Black, The 25
Briggs, Anne 125
Briggs, Raymond 77, 99
Bronson, Charles 42
Brontë, Charlotte 35n4
Brontë, Emily 18, 35n4
Brooker, Gary 95
Brown, Faith 20, 35n3
Buchan, John 64
Bush, Hannah 55, 85, 91
Bush, John 90
Bush, Paddy 25, 26, 37, 68, 85, 93, 114
Bush, Robert 59, 85
Butch Cassidy and the Sundance Kid 29

Cabinet of Dr. Caligari, The 29
Cagney, James 22, 29
Campbell, Joseph 96–97, 109, 123
'Candle in the Wind' 71
Canterbury Tale, A 86, 109–110
Capote, Truman 27
Captain Beefheart 94
Cardiff, Jack 100
Carnival of Souls 44
Carroll, Lewis 108–109
Castaway 39, 104
'Casting the Runes' 109
Chaney, Lon 22
Chaplin, Charlie 107–108, 113

Chorus Line, A 103, 110
Christmas Carol, A 34
Citizen Kane 9, 73
Clapton, Eric 88, 90
Clayton, Jack 26–27, 109
'Cloudbusting' 56–61, 62n12, 62n13, 68, 69, 70, 113
Cocteau Twins 36n7
Cocteau, Jean 74, 109
'Coffee Homeground' 23–24
Coltrane, Robbie 42, 46n3, 74–75
Come Back Kate 82n10
Comic Relief 20, 41, 95
Comic Strip Presents, The 11, 41–46, 70, 71, 74, 104, 112, 127
'Confrontation, The' 42
'Constellation of the Heart' 94, 97
Coogan, Steve 20
Cooper, Alice 97n2
Coppola, Francis Ford 11, 30, 34, 87, 127
Cornford, Lily 92, 109, 116
Creme, Lol 61n7
Cronenberg, David 11, 75
Cross of Iron 52
Cruel Sea, The 34
Crying Game, The 104, 112
Curse of Frankenstein, The 51
Curtis, Tony 28

Damage 104
David, Hal 37
Davis Jr., Sammy 24
Davis, Neil 30
Day of the Jackal, The 20
'Deeper Understanding' 46n3, 74–76, 127
'Delius (Song of Summer)' 25, 36n7, 117
Delius, Frederick 25–26, 53, 125
Denham, Maurice 32
Deren, Maya 107
Diaghilev, Sergei 100, 114
Dickens, Charles 34
Die Hard 42
Dinosaur 40
Director's Cut 74, 76, 91, 97n8, 119
Disney, Walt 11, 21, 22, 31, 40, 94, 99, 108, 127
'Don't Give Up' 61n7, 117

Don't Look Now 58, 109, 115, 131
Donner, Richard 66
Donohoe, Amanda 39
Double Indemnity 28
Doyle, Julian 57, 60, 61n10, 62n13, 104
Doyle, Margarita 104
Dr. Crippen 23
Dracula: Prince of Darkness 51
Dreaming, The (album) 4, 27, 36n9, 53, 55, 85, 125
'Dreaming, The' (song) 27–28, 55, 120
Duffer, Matt and Ross 1–2
Duffield, Bill 85
Dulac, Germaine 107
Dune 69

Easdale, Brian 100
'Eat the Music' 90–91, 97, 104, 109, 120–122
Edmondson, Ade 41
'Eider Falls at Lake Tahoe' 78
Eliot, T.S. 128
Elvis – Aloha From Hawaii 73
Empire Strikes Back, The 132
Enrico, Robert 44
Exorcist, The 92
'Experiment IV' 67–70, 75, 81n3, 82n5, 111
Eyes Wide Shut 74

Fabulous Baker Boys, The 61n2
Fairbanks, Douglas 87
Family Plot 70
Felicia's Journey 82n7
Fellini, Federico 43
Fenby, Eric 25, 36n7
Fielding, Noel 20, 75
Fire and Sword 92
Fisher, Terence 51
Fleming, Ian 20
Fleming, Victor 108
'Flower of the Mountain' 74
Forsyth, Frederick 20
French, Dawn 41, 68
Freud, Sigmund 57
Front Line 30
Fullerton, Alexander 21

Gabriel, Peter 53, 61n7, 117, 121
Gang's All Here, The 90

Garbo, Greta 4
Garfath, David 56, 62n13, 79, 82n14
'Get Out of My House' 31–32, 72, 129
Gilliam, Terry 11, 37, 38, 44, 56, 57, 59, 60, 75, 76, 78, 104, 130
Gilmour, Dave 13n1, 31, 37, 71
Gish, Lillian 107
GLC: The Carnage Continues ... 41–42
Godard, Jean-Luc 3
Godfather, The 34–35
Godley, Kevin 61n7
Gold Diggers, The 107, 124n6
Gold Rush, The 107
Golden Compass, The 40–41
Goldfinger 21
Golding, William 33
Goldman, William 29
Gone to Earth 33, 63, 65, 86, 101
Graceland 121
Graffiti Park 92
Graham, Martha 55–56
Grant, Cary 24, 131
Gray-Cullert, Dyane 55–56
Great Northfield Minnesota Raid, The 21
Gurdjieff, George 125

Hall, Roger 104
Halliwell-Phillips, James 32
'Hammer Horror' 22–23, 49, 110
Happy Days 80–81, 82n15, 85
Harry Potter and the Deathly Hallows: Part 1 78–79
Harry, Debbie 75
'Heads We're Dancing' 5
Heckroth, Hein 100
'Hello Earth' 34
Helpmann, Robert 102, 110
Henry, Lenny 95, 103
Henry, Paul 29, 55
Her 75–76
Herbert, Frank 69
Herrmann, Bernard 69
Hervieu, Michael 56, 61n9
Herzog, Werner 34
Hiller, Wendy 95
Hitchcock, Alfred 11, 25, 33, 56, 63–65, 69–70, 81n2, 86, 113, 115, 128, 131

144 Index

Hollow, Bob 104
'Home for Christmas' 42, 46n5
'Houdini' (song) 28
Houdini (film) 28
Houdini, Harry 28
Hounds of Love (album) 1, 32, 33, 46n1, 55, 56, 66, 72, 79
Hounds of Love (film) 36n12
'Hounds of Love' (song) 32–33, 63–66, 110, 113
Hughes, John 11, 39, 40
Hunchback of Notre Dame, The 22
Hurst, Gary 29, 85, 87

I Know Where I'm Going! 86, 95–96, 109
Idylls of the King 33
'If the Bomb Drops' 53
'In Search of Peter Pan' 22, 41, 99
Incredibles, The 90
'Infant Kiss, The' 26–27
Innocents, The 26, 109
Irvine, Lucy 39
Islander, The 39

Jacob's Ladder 44
'James and the Cold Gun' 20–21, 35n5
James, Henry 26
James, M.R. 109
Jane Eyre 35n4
Jesse James 21
Joan of Arc 72, 129
'Joanni' 72, 129
John, Elton 71
Johns, W.E. 69
Jones, Jennifer 33, 65
Jordan, Neil 75
Jovovich, Milla 72
Joyce, James 70–71, 74, 82n6
Jungle Book, The 94

Kafka, Franz 38
Kagemusha 130
Kamen, Michael 38, 91
'Kashka from Baghdad' 24, 35n6
Kate Bush Live at the Hammersmith Odeon 50, 55
Kate Bush Live on Stage 35n5
Kelly, Gene 103, 115

Kelly, Jon 97n1
Kemp, Lindsay 5, 55, 104, 105, 109, 114–116, 119
'Ken' 11, 25, 42, 46n4, 91, 127
Kennedy, Nigel 69, 82n5, 94
Kick Inside, The 18, 21, 115
'King of the Mountain' 72–73, 76
King, Stephen 31
Kingsland, Gerald 39
Kipling, Rudyard 94
Kirk, Richard 50
'Kite' 21
Kneale, Nigel 11, 70, 77
Korda, Alexander 100
Kovac, Robin 19
KT Bush Band, The 20, 51, 71
KT Fellowship, The 80
Kubrick, Stanley 4, 11, 31–32, 36n11, 43, 69, 74, 127, 131
Kurosawa, Akira 130

La Rivière du Hibou 44
Ladykillers, The 29
'Lake Tahoe' 78–79, 80, 82n12, 104
Laurie, Hugh 68
Lavender Hill Mob, The 29
Lawrence, D.H. 91
Lawson, Arthur 100
Leigh, Janet 28
Lenny Henry Show, The 95
Lenny Live and Unleashed 103
Lenya, Lotte 23
Les Dogs 11, 43–46, 49, 71, 127
Life and Death of Colonel Blimp, The 86
'Lily' 81, 92–93, 94, 97, 104, 116–117
Line, The Cross & The Curve, The 3, 11–12, 25, 55, 88, 89, 90, 92, 93, 94, 95, 96, 97, 98–124, 128
Lionheart (album) 21–22, 24, 36n9, 41, 54
Lionheart (film) 21
Lipa, Dua 36n10
Live and Let Die 122
Livesey, Roger 95
Livingstone, Ken 42
Love & Basketball 46n2
'Love and Anger' 46n4, 71, 114
Love You Till Tuesday 71
Lowell, Robert 128

Lucas, George 97
Lynch, David 69, 74, 116
'Lyra' 40–41

M*A*S*H 131
MacMillan, Keith 19, 25, 49–51, 55, 80, 115
Madonna 126
'Magician' 37–38
Magician of Lublin, The 37–38, 73
Man Called Otto, A 46n2
'Man I Love, The' 61n7
Man of a Thousand Faces 22, 36n11
'Man with the Child in His Eyes, The' 13n2, 49–50, 116, 127
Mankowitz, Gered 21–22
Marceau, Marcel 119
Marnie 25
Mary Poppins 66
Massine, Léonide 101, 114
Matter of Life and Death, A 86, 92
Maxwell 46n2
Mayall, Rik 41
McInnerny, Tim 43, 71
McIntosh, Albert 41, 72, 74, 88
McIntosh, Danny 88, 95, 111
McKenna, Siobhán 71, 82n6
Mercer, Bob 3, 20
Meshes of the Afternoon 107
Messenger: The Story of Joan of Arc, The 72
Metropolis 56
Miranda, Carmen 91
'Mistraldespair' 77–78
'Misty' 77, 99
Mitchell, David 82n13
Mitchell, Joni 4, 129
'Moments of Pleasure' 46n5, 74, 86, 87, 89, 91, 94, 104, 114, 118–119, 128
Monroe, Marilyn 71
Monty Python's Flying Circus 38, 52, 57, 81n4, 104, 130
Moonraker 37
Moorcock, Michael 94
Moore, Julianne 75
Moore, Roger 37
Moreau, Jeanne 26
'Mother Stands for Comfort' 33, 129
Mother, The 46n2

'Moving' 115
Muldaur, Geoff 38
Murakami, Jimmy 73, 77
Murphy, Alan 85–86, 87, 88
Myers, Stanley 39

Never for Ever 24, 36n7, 51, 53, 85
Newman, Paul 29, 56
Nielsen, Brigitte 42
Night of the Demon 32, 63, 64, 109, 131
'Night of the Swallow' 28
Nightingale, Florence 68
Nijinsky, Vaslav 100
'Ninth Wave, The' 33–34, 44, 79, 80, 82n13, 91, 129
North By Northwest 64
Northern Lights 40
Nosferatu the Vampyre 34
Not I 75
Notorious 131

'Occurrence at Owl Creek Bridge, An' 44, 46n6
'Oh England My Lionheart' 21
'One Last Look Around the House Before We Go' 42
Oram, Daphne 27
Other Sides 2, The 4
Other Sides, The 68, 82n9

Palin, Michael 130
Palmer, Del 28, 37, 67, 68, 85, 88, 95, 104
Panorama 53
Paths of Glory 69
Paxman, Jeremy 53
Peacock, Danny 43
Peckinpah, Sam 43, 52
Peeping Tom 86
Pendergrass, Teddy 95
Pennebaker, D.A. 4–5, 103
Performance 59
Peter Pan 22, 42, 66, 99
Pethig, Hazel 104
Pfeiffer, Michelle 61n2
Pincher Martin 33
Pink Floyd 31, 38, 53, 56, 71, 125
Pinocchio 21, 22, 31, 131
Placebo 13n1
Planer, Nigel 41

146 *Index*

Plath, Sylvia 85
Play School 66
Pleasence, Donald 23
Pose 12–13n1
Potter, Sally 107, 124n6, 128
Powell, Michael 3, 11, 33, 36n13, 85, 86–87, 89, 91, 92, 93, 94, 95, 98, 99, 100, 101, 102, 103, 106, 109, 110, 113, 114, 115, 117, 118–119, 122, 123, 128
Pratt, Roger 78, 104
Presley, Elvis 73
Pressburger, Emeric 3, 33, 36n13, 85, 86–87, 89, 93, 95, 100, 102, 103, 109, 115, 123, 128
Prince 88, 92, 94, 95, 97n7, 103
Procol Harum 95
Psycho 33, 69, 81n2, 130
'Pull Out the Pin' 4, 30–31
Pullman, Philip 40
Pureton, Gary 77
Purple Rain 103

Quatermass 70
Quatermass Experiment, The 70

Raft, George 29
Raiders of the Lost Ark 70
Raven – Swordsmistress of Chaos 50
Red Shoes, The (album) 3, 8, 11, 25, 46n5, 72, 74, 81, 85–97, 98, 99, 103–104, 115, 121, 122–123, 128
Red Shoes, The (film) 3, 32, 36n13, 73, 86, 89 90, 92, 98, 100–103, 106, 108, 109, 110, 114, 117, 119–120, 121, 123n1
Red Shoes, The (Korean film), 100
'Red Shoes, The' (song) 5, 58, 93–94, 97, 104, 113–114, 117, 120, 122, 124n8
'Red Shoes, The' (story) 89, 92, 99–101, 118
Redford, Robert 29
Reed, Oliver 39
Reich, Peter 57–59
Reich, Wilhelm 57–59, 62n11, 62n12, 75
Reid, Beryl 41
Reiniger, Lotte 11, 78
Renoir, Jean 26

Revolution 58
Rhys, Jean 35n4
Richardson, Miranda 43, 104, 105, 106, 112–113, 119
Richardson, Peter 37, 41, 42, 43, 45, 71, 112, 119
Richens, Pete 43
Rickman, Alan 42
Robin Hood: Prince of Thieves 92
Robin of Sherwood 92
Robinson, Edward G. 29
'Rocket Man' 71–72, 82n8, 82n9, 104
Rodd, Julian 104
Roeg, Nicolas 11, 23, 28, 39, 40, 58, 59, 104
Root of All Evil 101
Rosenthal, Joe 67
'Rubberband Girl' 46n5, 74, 90, 94, 104, 110–112, 120
'Running Up That Hill' 1–3, 12, 55–57, 62n13, 67, 80, 90, 110, 113, 115
Russell, Ken 11, 25, 91, 127

Saboteur 113
'Sam Lowry's First Dream (Brazil)' 38
Sanders, George 94
Sasdy, Peter 18, 70
'Sat in Your Lap' 5, 55
Saturday Night Live 13n2, 61n2
Saunders, Jennifer 41, 42
Scorsese, Martin 87
Scrooge 34
'Sea of Honey, A' 72
Seashell and the Clergyman, The 107
Secret Policeman's Third Ball, The 13n1
Selznick, David O. 33
Sensual World, The (album) 11, 34, 35, 40, 70, 74, 85, 87
'Sensual World, The' (song) 41, 70–71, 74, 82n7, 95
Seven Samurai 130
Shaft 42
Sharp, Cecil 50
Shearer, Moira 73, 100, 101, 106, 110
She-Ra: Princess of Power 50
She's Having a Baby 39–40, 71
Shining, The (film) 31–32, 43
Shining, The (novel) 31

'Shoedance' 124n8
Shout, The 81n4
Silent Movie 119
Simon, Paul 121
Singer, Isaac Bashevis 37
Singin' in the Rain 103, 115
'Sky of Honey, A' 72
'Snowflake' 4
Snowman, The 77–78
Some Like It Hot 71
'Song of Solomon, The' 91–92, 93
Song of Summer 25
'Sovay' 50
Spears, Britney 61n2
Stanwyck, Barbara 28
Star Wars 97, 132
Stephenson, Pamela 61n5
Stevens, Wallace 112
Stone Tape, The 70
Stranger Things 1–2, 3, 107, 124n9
Superman 66
'Suspended in Gaffa' 28–29, 55
Suspiria 123n2
Sutherland, Donald 58–59, 131
Swan Lake 25
Sweeney, The 9, 24

Tales of Hoffmann, The 86
Taupin, Bernie 71
Taylor, Elizabeth 107
Tchaikovsky, Pyotr 25
Tennyson, Alfred Lord 33
Thatcher, Margaret 42
'Them Heavy People' 13n2, 50, 51, 61n5, 71, 125
'Theme From *Shaft*' 42
'There Goes a Tenner' 29–30, 55, 85
Thief of Bagdad, The 87
This Was a Woman 101
'This Woman's Work' 35, 39–40, 46n2, 71, 74, 127
Thompson, Tommy 77
Through the Looking-Glass 108–109
Time Bandits 57, 58, 130–131
Tin Machine 87
To Kill a Mockingbird 131
'Top of the City' 94
Top of the Pops 19, 60, 70

Torn Curtain 56, 115
'Tour of Life' 5, 13n4, 20, 22, 24, 26, 37, 50, 85, 87
Tourneur, Jacques 32, 64, 109, 128
Truffaut, François 25–26, 65
Turn of the Screw, The 26
Twilight Zone, The 46n6, 124n10
Two Rooms 71

Ulysses (novel) 70–71, 82n6
Ulysses (film) 70
Unnamable, The 117
Utah Saints 61n10

Vampire Diaries, The 13n1
Van Cleef, Lee 42
van Laast, Anthony 22
Videodrome 75
Visconti, Tony 36n9
Vogler, Christopher 97

W.R.: Mysteries of the Organism 62n11
'Waking the Witch' 34, 46n3, 112
Walk Away and I Stumble 46n2
Walkabout 28
Walker, Tim 74
Watching You Without Me 34
Wax, Ruby 41, 42
Webb, Mary 33
'Wedding List, The' 25–26, 45
Weill, Kurt 23
Weitz, Chris 11, 40–41
Welles, Orson 73
Wenders, Wim 92–93, 97n4, 117, 128
Whole Story, The 61n3, 67, 69, 81n2
'Why Should I Love You?' 94–95, 121
Wide Sargasso Sea 35n4
'Wild Man' 76–77
Wild Turkey 42–43
Wilder, Billy 11, 28, 71
Willis, Bruce 42
Wings of Desire 92, 94, 117
Wiseman, Brian 55
Witchfinder General 34
Wizard of Oz, The 108
Women in Love 91

Woolrich, Cornell 25
Worth, Harry 50
'Wow' 24, 50, 51, 61n3
Wright, Richard 71
Wrong Trousers, The 105
Wuthering Heights (novel) 18–20, 35n4
Wuthering Heights (serial) 18–20, 70

'Wuthering Heights' (song) 3, 4, 11, 18–20, 21, 27, 32, 35n2, 49, 67, 70, 79, 80–81, 127

'You're the One' 95–96

Ziggy Stardust and the Spiders From Mars 4–5, 6, 103, 123n3

For Product Safety Concerns and Information please contact our EU representative GPSR@taylorandfrancis.com
Taylor & Francis Verlag GmbH, Kaufingerstraße 24, 80331 München, Germany

www.ingramcontent.com/pod-product-compliance
Lightning Source LLC
Chambersburg PA
CBHW071821230426
43670CB00013B/2530